My Road to Mandalay

Compiled from his father's letters

by David Townsend

Clink
Street

Published by Clink Street Publishing 2022

Copyright © 2022

First edition.

The author asserts the moral right under the Copyright, Designs and Patents Act 1988 to be identified as the author of this work.

ISBN:
978-1-913962-87-6 - paperback
978-1-913962-88-3 - ebook

For George, Sophia and Arlo.
Do the best that you can at whatever you do.

This story, told by your Great Grandfather,
sets a fine example of doing just that.

*Sincere thanks to Sally Townsend for providing
the illustrations included within this book*

Contents

Foreword

David Townsend

Signing up on his 20th Birthday on the 13th June 1940, my father embarked on a journey, through the Second World War that would last until his homecoming from Burma in July 1946. In that time he would start 'in the sand' in North Africa, would gain a commission in the Indian Army and would become a specialist in tank transport, providing tanks and ammunition to the front line in the Battle of Imphal; a battle that lasted for four months between March to July 1943 and cost over 60,000 lives.

When the move south to 'retake Burma' started he was seconded to the 19th "Dagger" Division under the enigmatic leader, Major General 'Napoleon' Rees and, having delivered both Tanks and Gurkhas to their forward positions, would be one of the first two 'Service Wallahs' into Mandalay . A further secondment to the 2nd British Division would see him arrive in Rangoon shortly after its fall in March 1945. Here he would 'save the General', ensuring that the next Governor of Burma was not late for his first meeting with Admiral Lord Louis Mountbatten, 'the Supremo'.

These and other equally surprising stories are told with a sense of humour, with an appreciation of the countries and of the people and very often without due regard for the evident dangers that were all around. At heart it is an adventure. A young man in his twenties visiting lands that he would never otherwise have visited. Leading convoys for 1200 miles across India before he was 23 and becoming a Major when still only 25.

Perhaps a quote from April '44 will give you some idea of what is to come:

" We've Japs on three sides, the main road to the outside world is our (*only*) exit; we live just the same, eat just the same (and will go on eating OK for months and months and even if the grub should run low it's dropped like manna from heaven – good old RAF), drink wallop, write home and work just the same – and boy we've got some lovely guns."

Yet, in the same month he writes : " Quite a bit of mail has arrived including the Income Tax quiz! Imagine, here's us with Japs three miles away in one direction, being soothed to sleep each night by the comforting sound of our guns and some twerp manages to find a form which asks, 'Do you reside abroad for the sake of your health?' and 'Do you claim to be a British subject – if so on what grounds?', 'Are you a member of a missionary society?!'

From a personal perspective the amazing thing was that so little of this story had been learned from the man himself. I knew that he had served at least in part in Burma. I knew he had been involved in convoys and tank transport but very little else – except that his bad back, a constant problem, was the result of "riding in a jeep over dire roads for too many years." He, like many others returning from Burma, chose not to share his tales.

In 2011, while clearing out my mother's loft we found a 'hoard' of letters. There were over 500. The majority written to my father's family but over 100 written to one Connie Pead, a stranger, who became his pen-friend early in 1944 and later became his wife. It was not until the Covid lockdowns of 2020 that there was time to give these letters the attention that they deserved. It became an all-consuming project which provided an excellent diversion from the many restraints and difficulties posed by the pandemic. A group of friends as well as family eagerly awaited the instalments as they became available and from that this volume has now emerged.

The battles fought between 1943 and 1945 to regain control of Burma from the Japanese have often been referred to as 'The Forgotten War' fought by 'The Forgotten Army'. This story brings to life just what it was like to be there from start to finish. It is not a story of 'blood and guts'. It is the story of a young man from a very unassuming background, growing up fast, readily accepting all responsibilities put his way in very challenging circumstances and living the adventure to the full. The re-take of Burma is certainly a part of the Second World War that has received less publicity than it deserves.

I hope that you enjoy reading this whole extraordinary story as much as I have enjoyed putting it together.

PART 1

Laying the Foundations

June 1940 – April 1942

Private D.A. Townsend, Egypt 1941

CHAPTER 1

Setting the Scene

INTRODUCTION

Part One of this story will take you from the date that Dad joined the army on his 20th birthday, the 13th June 1940, through his training in Yorkshire, his first assignments in Aldershot and Barry Island in South Wales and then on to Egypt.

As he arrives in Egypt he starts on the banks of the Bitter Lakes near Suez where the Germans are laying mines each night. After just a few weeks he is posted to Benghazi but, as Erwin Rommel surprises all with the speed of his advance from Tripoli, he is asked to return. By the time he returns, orders have been issued for the majority of his regiment to be posted to Greece. In his absence someone else has filled his spot; that stroke of fate, missing that posting to Greece, changed his whole future war experience.

Within weeks a new assignment follows, working in the Transport Logistics Department at Middle East HQ in Cairo. He will stay here for a year, supporting the needs of the Western Desert Campaign and the 8th Army in their attempts to overcome the ingenuity of Rommel and the strength of his Panzer divisions. A year which would see the pendulum of success move both ways, with the most decisive battles at El Alamein yet to come.

Whilst the Desert Campaign in Africa was continuing British forces had suffered their biggest ever retreat in Burma. The Japanese had attacked Rangoon in December 1941 and by the middle of 1942 there were no longer any Allied troops left on Burmese soil. The 900 miles from Rangoon in the south to the safety of India in the north had cost more than 13,000 British and Indian casualties.

The Allies were now regrouping, rebuilding their forces to retake Burma and were seeking to increase the number of British Officers in the Indian Army. Seeing a related bulletin for such recruits, Dad applied for a commission in the Indian Army in January '42. He was successful and this section finishes with him catching a boat in April '42 destined for Bombay (now Mumbai) and an incredible adventure. Still only 21, he was the youngest of 25 successful applicants that had been selected. The true adventure had now begun.

THE WAR IN EUROPE IN JUNE 1940

To set the scene, first a little about what was happening as Dad joined up. Just tw
weeks before he signed up on the 13ᵗʰ June 1940, the evacuation of Dunkirk ha
taken place. It had been nine months since Germany had invaded Poland, on 1
September 1939, and although the period up to the spring of 1940 had been quie
enough, things were now going dramatically wrong from a British perspective.

By the end of 1939 Poland had effectively been divided up between German
and their collaborator, Russia. Britain introduced food rationing in January 194
but for the most part, time was spent in preparing for what was expected to come
The term 'the phoney war' which was often applied to this period, was well earned

Things began to heat up when Germany invaded both Norway and Denmar
in April 1940. Denmark surrendered but Norway, with support from Britain
and France, did not. On 10ᵗʰ May, the same day as Winston Churchill replace
Neville Chamberlain as British Prime Minister, Germany invaded France
Belgium and Holland. This was the start of the 'Blitzkrieg' or 'lightning war
Germany's combination of fast armoured tanks on land and superiority in th
air was devastating. They quickly overcame the superior numbers of French an
Belgium forces, even though the British Expeditionary Force had been sent t
help them.

Holland and Belgium fell by the end of May and by the 27ᵗʰ the evacuatio
from Dunkirk had started. So, by the time my father signed up on the 13ᵗʰ June i
was all happening! On the day after he signed up, on 14ᵗʰ June, Paris would fall

Joining the Royal Army Service Corp (RASC)

It is not surprising that, with all that was going on, there were many who wante
to 'sign up' and 'do their bit'. It is clear too that by 'volunteering' there was a
element of choice as to which of the services you could join.

Dad chose to go into the Royal Army Service Corp (RASC), the prime functio
of which is more aligned to 'Services and Supply' than to direct combat. A sectio
of the Army where he evidently thought that his work experience, as a clerk in loca
government, could be better utilised than being a 'man at arms'. By the time th
six years covered by this story are over however, any thought of this being a 'sof
option' can be firmly dismissed!

THE ONGOING WAR: JULY – DECEMBER 1940

Whilst Dad was undertaking his initial Army training, the Battle of Britain was getting underway. This started in July and was the first battle to be fought solely in the air. Keep this in mind as you read of 'air raid duties' in the coming pages.

Britain secured a first narrow but hugely important victory. Britain had more planes than the Germans but not as many pilots and the heroics of the pilots we did have, coupled with radar, were all important to our success. As a consequence by the end of October Hitler called off his planned UK invasion.

As the Battle of Britain concluded The Blitz commenced. This was the term given to the systematic bombing of British cities. Amongst the first properties to be affected was Dad's home address in Walthamstow E17. It would be a full year before there was once again 'a family home' in that area.

And so to the letters

As far as possible the whole story is copied direct from 'the letters' and the date of the letter is given as part of the heading. Where the writing is mine, such as this chapter and the occasional note or explanation, then I have used italics. These additions will hopefully assist understanding, provide useful background and help to put things into context.

CHAPTER 2

Initial Training and First Assignments

June – December 1940

JUNE '40

Sign Up Papers
These were signed on 13th June 1940.

JULY / AUGUST '40

SOWERBY BRIDGE Training Camp – Yorkshire
July / Aug 1940 (2 undated letters)

Settling In

I have now really settled down and have hardly anything to complain about. The Officers, NCO's and instructors are all nice fellows, no bullies, always ready to help. So far, I have not come across one chap who has not been decent to get on with even though I mix with about 500 a day.

The variety of chaps here is amazing. There are lots of Scots and Welshmen and every town in England seems to be represented. I still find it hard to understand an Irishman and a Scot having an argument – they always seem to be in such earnest. Possibly they do not understand each other, anyway.

The Routine

We have to get up at six each morning and be washed, shaved, dressed, have bed made, blankets and great coat folded, kit ready for inspection and boots and buttons polished and be on the parade ground by 6.45.

Breakfast at 7.30, parade at 8.20, dinner at 12.45, parade 1.15, tea 5.10 and the rest of the time is ours. Most of our spare time is spent on cleaning. The rifle has to be cleaned daily and we have drilled with it until our hands are sore.

Each morning and afternoon is divided into four periods and include foot drill, rifle drill, weapons training and PT with occasional sessions on map reading, gas lectures and later on, driving instruction. Our training officially started last Tuesday, and we have been told that if we are good at our drills and training, we will leave in a month, if not, any time after that.

Air Raid Warnings

I mentioned the air raid warning on Monday night. Well, we had one on Tuesday and again on Thursday. It seems we are called up at the yellow warnings and we never have had a red. *(Yellow coding was for 'wardens to gather at their posts – public not informed', red was 'air raid imminent' and Green 'raid has passed'.)*

Nevertheless, dressing at any time between 12 and 4 am is no fun so we are told we can go back to sleep fully dressed. I have it to a fine art and last night was asleep in five minutes (no bed and with a kit bag for a pillow)!

Food and Fatigues

We have just had breakfast (2 sausages apiece and no complaints). They seem very fond of giving us tinned tomatoes – we have them at least 3 or 4 times a week, with bacon for breakfast. Food in fact is easy to get. If you feel very hungry you just get on the end of the table and help serve. As there are about 30 men to each table and no control of the dishes it is easy to get one or two extra and then share them out. Clever what!

We have now started regular fatigues, every fourth day. I mentioned Friday's washing up; that was not too bad. Even better was on Monday when we went to the baths – I was near the front and I and another chap were detailed to be bath orderlies for the afternoon. We had to fill the baths, empty when finished, clean out and fill again. I missed all the drills for the afternoon and was sweating away in the baths wearing trousers and boots only. Picture me like this telling the Company Sergeant Major (CSM) that his bath was ready. I found it hard to keep a straight face.

To make up for this work, I picked the best bath, with shower attached and spent three quarters of an hour wallowing. It was really good, especially as I had been tipping the other fellows out after about ten minutes.

And as things continue

Marching has now become automatic; in fact, we look like a chain gang at a prison. Rifle drill is one of the most tiring periods, mine weighs about 10lbs and to hold it in any one position for long becomes painful.

We have started PT and I am beginning to feel the effects of it. We have all sorts of exercises and games and today we are going to have boxing lessons. At first it makes your legs as stiff as boards but later it just makes a pleasant change from drilling.

I have now to parade, with tin hat, gas mask and rifle – the morning's work.

Training was satisfactorily completed without further incident and the next posting was to Aldershot.

SEPTEMBER '40

ALDERSHOT
9-09-40

Please excuse my silence recently but things have been moving fast and it has left me rather staggered.

To begin at the beginning. The office I was in was known as the 'Training Company and P.A.D. [*Passive Air Defence*] Office'. Last Saturday a new captain arrived to take charge of the Training Company and when he arrived, he just sacked the existing officers on the spot, describing their training system in good Army language. He refused to take over the P.A.D. and so transferred the officers to put them in charge of all air raid duties, he himself dealing with training only.

The sergeant under whom I was working was also taken and the captain asked me if I could do his job. I said I could and was made chief clerk on the spot and now I have to pick out men for guards, fatigues and everything else. We have no typewriter or duplicator but even so, by borrowing and 'using for a few minutes', I have so far managed to print the orders (30 copies) each day.

By the looks of things, I am due to get a few stripes when the company is established because now I have three chaps under me but of course everything could flop and we'll all go back to the square. Even so, it's good fun being at the centre of things. The Captain (only about 30) knows what he wants and means to get it.

I tackled him about the 'Duty Clerk' job, which means sleeping in the office and being wakened by every air raid warning. He went into the matter and found that our main job was to be on the spot to call out defence platoons should an invasion occur. So, we still have to sleep in the office, but no more phone calls, so I will sleep in peace.

So don't worry about me, I mean to settle in to 'my new position' – it's surprising how popular one becomes when you have to put the guards on etc..

"I say old chap, could you arrange that I don't go on guard over the week end as it's my wedding anniversary," or "You might fix it so that I go on leave the same time as so and so."

Duties continued at Aldershot until a posting to Barry Island, South Wales in November '40.

NOVEMBER '40

BARRY ISLAND
Undated: 'Wednesday Dinner Time'

Address: RASC, No 4 section, Draft RCIHC, Barry, Wales

Please note change of address and new draft. This draft is called the 'Tiger Draft' which makes me the youngest cub.

We have all settled down well – straw paillasses [*a mattress consisting of a thin pad filled with straw or sawdust*] over wire beds, paraffin oil heater and have treated ourselves to enamel mugs and plates to help the food go down better. The food has improved, the weather has improved, and everything is rosy. In fact, we are all enjoying ourselves.

The locals apologised for the weather we had the first two days, since then it has been lovely, and we went rock climbing yesterday in glorious sunshine. A destroyer and a large liner were anchored opposite our little bay and we went out as far as possible over the rocks to see them – I might add that they left during the night, so we have no reason to go on the sand today.

I have been put in the office again and this time I have a captain and two lieutenants to look after. Today I have been dealing with pay. I seem to be going from strength to strength!

If I am lucky, I will stay in this office – the section office of No 4 detachment – until we get wherever we are going. It will suit me fine – no guards or other awkward fatigues.

Christmas Tales
27-12-40

I am sorry I did not mention Christmas in my last letter, but we had lost all account of time and I did not realise it was so close until after I had sent the news. I had better give you the programme as it occurred:

Christmas Eve a few of us had a night out in Barry Dock (quite a nice town!). Percy went to the café where we have palled up with the owner and on Christmas morning, he came up to me and whispered that we were invited out to tea – no complaints!

There was a church parade on Christmas morning, but I arranged that Percy, myself and another chap did not go on it. Instead, I found enough official business that had to be done in Barry and shared it amongst the three of us and we trooped down the road that connects the island to the mainland, convinced the guard that we were working and then went for a walk.

It was really fine – a beautiful day and we walked right along the coast and fitted in a bit of rock climbing to give us an appetite. We arrived back at barracks just in time for dinner – and what a dinner!

The most important thing is that we had tablecloths! The spread on them was A1. Plates of meat, dates, apples, oranges, a packet of cigarettes and a bar of chocolate for everyone ; – and BEER. The dinner itself was roast beef, roast pork, cabbage and roast potatoes, all served up by the officers, plus Christmas pudding (2 helpings) – and once again BEER.

Actually, I only had one mug of beverage and even then, by calling the Major, commanding the draft and ordering a bottle of lemonade from him (he had to fetch it himself!). I mixed myself a shandy and dined in style.

An hour and a half later when we were pouring out, they called for volunteers for washing up. As no one felt like it they were detailed (you, you and you) – I was the last 'you' but by a bit of clever work I walked up to the door of the washhouse and while the sergeant in charge was looking for some more mugs, I about turned and hopped it. No washing up so soon after dinner for me!

At four-o-clock we went to tea. I have seldom been made more at home by strangers – there were four soldiers and their wives staying in the rooms above the café and they and we (the three musketeers) were entertained marvellously.

Tea consisted of fruit salad, trifles, blancmange, jellies and cakes – then plenty of fun and at midnight, supper – a supper that could only be turned out by someone used to catering in style. Food, sweets and drinks if necessary were showered upon us and at one-o-clock Boxing Day we began to adjourn.

We could not repay them in any way, so we offered to do the washing up – just for fun – and so we turned ourselves into a fatigue party and cleared up in an amazingly efficient manner.

When we left, Mrs Ireland, our hostess, invited us to tea etc that night – it was already Boxing Day! We accepted but stipulated that we would arrive in time to wash up the dinner things and so Christmas Day ended by us tiptoeing into the billets at 1.45 am Boxing Day. I climbed up into my bunk, without waking the chap beneath.

On Boxing Day, we repeated the dose, arriving in time for washing up – then having a 'light' tea (mince pies, cakes, fruit salad etc.) and dinner at 9 pm. What a dinner (chicken, Christmas pud and all the frills)! It left us gasping and tired and eventually we got to bed at 2.30 this morning. Please note we are going to bed early tonight!

And yet another trick!

The smartest thing that has happened occurred at dinner on Christmas Day. An Officer got six men to carry two-quart bottles of beer each into the mess room. They were checked at the outside door and again inside, yet two bottles reposed in one of the beds in our billet after dinner!

What happened was that one of the boys, after being checked inside, turned round while no one was looking and marched out on the end of the file of men who were leaving – and no-one noticed his two bonnie babes!

Tropical kit issued

We have been issued with our tropical kit and today we are to collect 50 rounds of ammunition each – then we will have everything; ready to move at an hours' notice.

The most likely thing is that we will leave in the middle of the night by train for Glasgow and the Clyde (no troops leave Barry Docks!) The train doors are locked when you get in and you go straight on to the ship and are not allowed off again.

The office work is going well – all I am going to do today is sit by the officer and show the lads where to sign for their pay – tough job!

Time to leave
4 -1-41
We are leaving here today – at least our kit bags have gone – and we are to be paid again at 7o/c tonight. Destination is still unknown, rumour says Glasgow or Liverpool.

We will be terribly sorry to leave here. Last night was the first since Christmas that I had been in bed before midnight and that was because there was a role call at 10.30 pm. Mrs Ireland has given us the run of her house and café – I am writing this in the lounge – and we spend all our spare time here. I served up poached egg on toast for two customers today! We have been taken out to whist drives and socials and had a marvellous time.

Last Tuesday we went to a party at a church for the Sunday School teachers and boy, Sunday School teachers aren't all the vicars would like to think they are!

The next night one of Mrs Ireland's friends asked us out to tea and this was followed by a whist drive. Frank (the chap from Shropshire) won first gents prize and I got second. The prizes were cigarettes and as neither of us smoke the lads in our billet did rather well.

Sounds of war
Thursday's raid on Cardiff (7 miles away) did not affect us at all. Guns were going a lot and the nearest bomb fell a mile away, but it upset the locals a bit (It's the first heavy raid they have had.)

By the time of the next letter the UK has been left behind and the next stage of the adventure had begun.

CHAPTER 3

The Sea Journey to Egypt

January – March 1941

JANUARY '41

At Sea
17-1-41

For some time now I have been a sailor and so far, I am enjoying the experience (if only the ship would keep still)!

Sleeping in hammocks at night and gazing into the void during the day is now becoming a habit. So far, the sea has not been rough – but at times the well makes the ship pitch like a duck. Percy and Frank have both been seasick but yours truly is feeling fine.

We left Barry in style, marching out late at night wearing overcoats and topees [*pith helmets*]. Overcoats have since been discarded.

Travelling as we have been, our time has differed from yours and we have had to put our watches back two hours. The first hour was delayed a day or two and so we paraded at 9.30 one morning in the dark and were on deck at 8 pm in day light. That has since been remedied and the hours of daylight are back to normal.

FEBRUARY '41

Three weeks later – a port of call
5-2-41

The voice from the deep bids you all the very best. I can assure you that I am having the time of my life and spend half my time prowling round the ship looking for cool spots, while you, no doubt, are finding it difficult to keep warm.

Since I last wrote we have called at a port (to remain unknown per the censor).[1] It was in one of the world's hot spots and although we were there during the local winter, the heat at times was intense. The temperature on our mess deck was 130 degrees [*54 Centigrade!*] and we heard a delicious rumour, unconfirmed, that it was the coldest winter they had had for nine years.

We had previously changed into tropical kit and had been sleeping on deck but while in port no sleeping on deck was allowed owing to the danger of mosquitoes.

As soon as we arrived in port (well, anchored half a mile offshore), natives in their small canoes and boats soon surrounded our ship, selling oranges, bananas, pineapples, mangroves, other doubtful fruit, fish, eggs and baskets.

We had been warned not to buy anything from them, especially fruit, to avoid bringing disease aboard, so we concentrated on the entertainers. Their speciality was diving out of their light canoes and retrieving coins thrown into the water. It would appear that it is one of the most profitable jobs in the district because the competition is great.

All the natives speak very good English (or very bad if they dive after a shilling and find it is only a halfpenny covered with silver paper) and some bartering gets heated. The first diver to come alongside sang 'The Lambeth Walk 'and 'Tipperary', which of course made us ready to expect anything from the crowd that followed.

Happy to leave again

Although we had been glad to see land, it was with distinct relief that we left because the heat was a bit too great to be pleasant. Once out to sea again and everything was OK. Also, we had a daily dose of quinine while near land and we were not at all sorry to finish with that.

It is surprising how easy it is to fill our spare time. There is often something interesting to see over the side – flying fish, rainbows, passing ships and the phosphorescence of the water – but most of our time is spent either reading or playing cards. There is also plenty of entertainment provided – boxing, concerts, spelling bees and talent competitions. So, you can see that we don't find it monotonous.

When we crossed the Equator the 'crossing-the-line' ceremony was held. Father Neptune 'came aboard' and held a mock court which resulted in several chaps being shaved with a piece of wood and ducked in a canvas tank of water.

---

1   The port was Freetown, West Africa

The show piece was most unexpected, especially to the participants – a sergeant and a corporal were thrown in fully clothed – even wearing their topees and it provided the best laugh we have had.

A second port of call – three weeks later
27-2-41

I assure you that I have never felt (or looked) so healthy before. I have had some shore leave [*Durban*] and after being at sea for six weeks, the sight of cars and shops was a pleasant change.

We sighted land after breakfast and docked at 2 pm. From the sea the town looked impressive, with big modern buildings stretching right along the front, but when we went ashore at 6 pm, the lights and the size of the buildings took our breath away.

The buildings are anything up to 20 storeys high, every window alight. Neon signs, shops and streets are brilliant and car headlights simply blaze. I found later that there is hardly a chimney pot in the city – it is completely electrified – and do they make the most of it!

My pals (Percy and Frank) and I walked to the centre of the town, refusing all offers of sudden death in a rickshaw.

The transport situation is a strange mixture of old and new; rickshaws, pulled by curiously garbed natives, Bantus, and high powered, streamlined taxis – both are expensive if you don't haggle with the native. However, we just wandered and gazed and eventually got lost behind the town.

A car pulled up and the driver offered us a lift. He was an Indian and proved to be a wonderful chap. He had travelled all over England, India, and S. Africa and seemed to know London better than I. We were soon all eagerly discussing England as it is, as it was and will be and our host combined this with a drive around the town. He finally left us at a hotel with an invitation to dinner the following evening.

We then began to quench our slaked throats. A limit had been set at two pints of lager (iced) and it was not our fault that a third was set in front of us – really! We got into conversation with the chief engineer of a cargo boat, which had developed engine trouble while in convoy, then ran out of water for the boilers, eventually arriving in port with the boilers lined with salt, after using sea water.

The engineer was with a boiler repairer who seconded his story and was thirsty – so we did not offend and accepted the drinks. We had previously noticed that, after being on board for so long, we swayed slightly when standing still. This was cured! Everything else swayed – and we felt fine!

Back to the ship

Going back to the ship was an experience. Trolley buses and trams, being free to the troops, were packed; lines of cars were giving the boys lifts and rickshaws were everywhere (many with the owner in the seat and a soldier between the shafts).

The people of the town were amazing in their hospitality and most of our boys had invitations the next day. On arriving at our new friend's house, we were made completely at home. The people of the house speak English better than Indian and the exchange of news and ideas was exceedingly interesting.

In due course we were conducted, not unwillingly, to the food. It is hard to describe the feast – for it was a feast: soup, fish, ice cream, chicken, fruit salad and fresh fruit; all with the necessary etceteras; and, although they themselves were TT, Scotch and soda was provided. I must say my face is brown, not red, but it did go down well!

Another trip round the town in the car and being delivered to the ship (with 5 minutes to spare) was a wonderful finish to a perfect day, especially as it was accompanied by another invite, for the next day but one. This was lucky, for the next day I had to remain on board to act as a mess guard. Unpleasant, though it gave me the chance to do the weekly wash in peace.

The next day

Next day I was on deck with Percy when the 12 o/c hooter sounded and we were both determined to make up for the loss of the previous day. We started walking towards the hills that lay behind the town and by boarding the first tram that came along, succeeded in getting to the top of the hills in comfort.

The view and the coolness were marvellous. We had, unknowingly, arrived at one of the local attractions; a piece of bush country reserved as a sanctuary for birds and monkeys. Whether the locals appreciate the monkeys or not I don't know, for they often enter houses and help themselves, but they were amusing all the same.

Whilst we were studying their antics, a lady came up to us and invited us home to tea, and we, being full of 'entente cordiale' couldn't refuse. Time passed quickly and we found ourselves overdue for our next commitment. It was hard to refuse an invitation to stay but we were delivered back to town in a car (everyone seems to have a car even if they can't afford it).

The evening that followed was even more successful than before. During its course we were shown some of the saris worn by the Indian ladies. I have never seen such beautiful materials or colours; some of them covered in hand worked patterns of gold thread.

Yet another car ride followed, this time in the hills where we had been in the afternoon. The sight of the town ablaze below us 'beat Blackpool' according to those who had been there.

Arriving back at the ship we found that no more leave was allowed after midnight (it was 11.50) and so our brief but crowded stay ended.

To sea once again

We left the following evening, and being the last ship to leave, received the full blast of the city's send off. The hospitality of S E Africa will be remembered by us for a long time to come.

Since then, we have crossed 'the line' once more and should be arriving 'somewhere' soon.

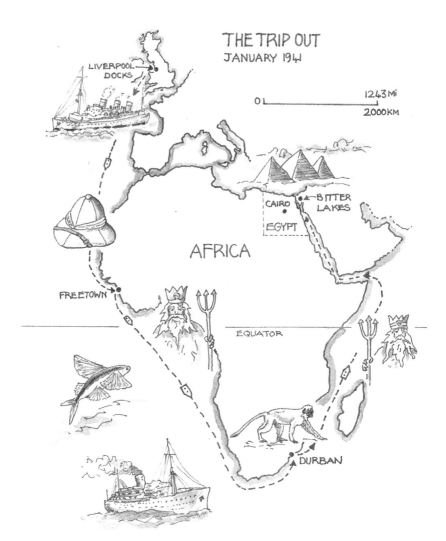

The Trip Out - January '41
© Sally Townsend

CHAPTER 4

The War in Africa up to 1941

It's worth spending a little time here explaining what was happening in the war in Africa as my father and his co-travellers arrived in March 1941. Remember that his ship was one of 20 liners in the convoy. This was one of the largest mobilisations of British troops that had ever been made in one go.

For their own reasons Italy and Japan had both decided to support Hitler and signed a three- way agreement with Germany in September 1940. Italy and Germany had signed an earlier agreement in 1936 with Benito Mussolini, the Italian dictator, declaring that "all other European powers would rotate on the Rome-Berlin axis." The term 'Axis' was now applied to the three powers combined.

Italy had established an 'East African Empire' in 1936 which included Somalia, Eritrea and Ethiopia and had considerable forces already in the region. As part of the Axis agreement North Africa therefore became their responsibility. They had invaded Egypt from Libya in September '40 and planned to work their way along the North Africa Coast to secure the Suez Canal.

After some initial success for the Italians the turning point for the Allies came in February '41 when the British Commander, Archibald Wavell, withdrew his forces into Egypt with the expectation that the Italians would over-extend their supply lines. It worked. Despite their hugely superior numbers the Italians were defeated and over 130,000 of them were taken prisoner by the British.

Whilst this was happening Hitler had a call for help from Mussolini and agreed to send a small armoured 'Panzer' division to assist. The head of this division was General Lieutenant Erwin Rommel. His orders were to 'protect Tripoli' and take further orders from the Italian commander, Italo Gariboldi.

By February 1941 Greece was the only ally that Britain had in Europe that had not yet succumbed to Hitler. However, the country was under pressure and sent an urgent plea for help to Churchill. Churchill, believing that the Italians were beaten in North Africa and more significantly, that any help that the Germans could give them was a long way off, ordered Wavell to send 58,000 troops to help the Greeks.

This was all happening just as Dad and others were arriving. You will read that Dad was posted to Benghazi, got as far as Alexandria and then was asked to return.

Rommel, who had arrived in North Africa a full month ahead of expectations, heard of the planned movement of troops to Greece and realised that this left the British short of resources. Contrary to his orders to 'protect Tripoli' he decided to march on Benghazi. He was incredibly successful. He overcame the British 3rd Armoured brigade at Mechill which led to the British retreat continuing past Benghazi toward Tobruk and then to the Libyan/Egyptian frontier. Benghazi fell on 3rd April, Cyrenaica on the 8th and only Tobruk remained in Allied hands.

From a seemingly victorious position at the end of February it had all changed six weeks later. By the 11th of April, Rommel had started 'The Siege of Tobruk' that was to last for 241 days.

As you read the letters that follow bear in mind that the reasons for the long hours of work 'back in the office' are for a very worthy cause – dealing with the supply and related problems of transport, while the East Africa campaign continued.

CHAPTER 5

A Year in Middle East HQ

March '41- April '42

MARCH '41

Arrival
12-03-41
We left the ship after being on board for nine weeks and one day, so we are glad of a change.

The train journey from the port to this camp was an experience. It gave us the first glance of the desert, mud-houses, eastern trains and hawkers. Somehow, as the train left the station it filled with natives, ages ranging from 9 to 90, all endeavouring to push goods into your hands and extract money from your pocket.

While waiting in the station, I had acted as a runner between the train and the canteen and so had got used to the currency. We therefore managed to haggle and get the best of the bargains. At least, the natives must still have made their profits, but we only paid a quarter of the first demand.

As we approached the camp all we could see was dozens of tents but now, having found our way around, we have found a NAAFI canteen and a cinema. Water is laid on (1/4 mile from our tent) and the grub's good. What more can we want in the desert!

The tents themselves are roomy and after sleeping on a hard deck, palliasses are a luxury.

APRIL '41

Transfer to GHQ
17-04-41
New Address: RASC, GHQ, ST (V), ME

I have delayed this letter because, until Sunday 13th, I was still at the base and there was not much to write about. Now I have been posted to GHQ and am starting Army clerking in earnest.

Life at the base was mostly sand and sun interspersed with 'spud-bashing', parades, guarding Italian prisoners, more parades, going to the cinema and even more parades. The parades were boring, 'spud-bashing' was dirty and the flicks were about 10 years old so guarding Wops was the most interesting thing that happened.

One bright spot in my five weeks stay was a posting that came through and was cancelled. I was sent on it and having got halfway to my 'promised land', was recalled. It seems the Germans reached my destination [*Benghazi*] before I did, so I was not unhappy to return.

My new job should prove interesting. ST stands for 'Supply and Transport'. V for 'Vehicles' – quite a big subject and as it is entirely new to me, means plenty of hard graft. We work in the morning and in the evening, having the afternoon off (because of the heat) and I am to have one day off a week.

There seems to be plenty of things to do in our spare time: e.g., visit Pyramids, zoo, cinemas, trams (the cheapest thing in the country) and sleep!

The best thing that has happened so far is that Percy and I have been kept together. Actually, he was posted three days before me and I met him the night I arrived, and we now work in adjoining offices! Frank was posted some time ago and we have lost touch with him, but it looks as though we will be holding re-unions all over England when the war ends.

MAY '41

One month in
3-05-41

It is rather strange that I keep meeting people I know. Wally Thorpe, Ted Lowton's pal came across on the same boat as me but being in a different Corps we have lost touch. Alf Jarmain sleeps in the next room to me and I have met several other chaps from Walthamstow.

We work 8–1.30 and nights 6–9.30, having the afternoons free but as the sun is so hot, we do little else but sleep after dinner. All my odd jobs get done on Saturdays when I am free all day.

Today is my third 'day off' and so far I have not arranged to go anywhere. The previous Saturdays have been spent mainly in going to the zoo and the cinema. (The seats at the flicks are wooden and they made their mark.) My next excursion will be to the Pyramids but climbing them inside and out is a warm and tiring business, so I am getting a reserve of energy first.

Incidentally, I have bought a camera, leaving myself almost broke, but it will give you some idea of what the country looks like. Most of the photos look rather good and create an impression of 'Romance of the East' – if only you could photograph smells!

My comments and views on the country are in the other letter and my views are the same as those of an officer to whom I was speaking (I use his words): "If it wasn't for the sand and the sun, the flies and the Egyptians, this country would be quite a nice place." However, it is good to be stationed in Cairo because we do not get quite so much sand or flies and have all the facilities and amusements of a big city at our disposal.

Heatwave!
15-05-4

I am getting on fine; my job is interesting; pals are pally and what spare time we do get is crammed. Last week we were subjected to a heat wave – the hottest Cairo has had in three years – and it makes us consider 90 degrees in the shade quite cool. The result was that our afternoons were spent sweating and sleeping (if the flies allowed). I have also spent 2 afternoons this week at lectures and one endeavouring to get two natives to clean the offices out, so my spare time has always started at 9.30pm.

There is only a partial blackout and plenty to do and see at nights. Cinemas open 10 pm–12.30 and the streets are still busy at 1am which is the latest I have been or want to be out. We go to a handy café owned by a Greek and patronised by every possible nationality, always plenty of atmosphere!

Thanks again for the offer to send out things but it is really not needed while I am working here. We can get all we need and are constantly being offered things we don't want; we know all the right words and soon manage to clear away the street pedlars.

31-05-41

Everything here is still going fine. The weather is not so hot. My pal Percy has been posted and the three Musketeers are now spread all over the map. I have palled up with a Glasgow chap who is almost understandable – a bit different to a chap with whom I work, from Falkirk, he seems to have a language all of his own. However, we are a happy gang and as I said, everything is fine.

JUNE '41

Operation 'Battle Axe' approaches2
8-06-41

We now only get half a day off each week, but I used mine to advantage and visited the Pyramids. That is just about as far as I got, for having arrived mid-afternoon I contented myself by gazing upward, postponing the climb until Autumn or Winter, whichever comes sooner out here!

It was though an exceedingly enjoyable afternoon and I can understand why some of the mummies are supposed to wander round at the dead of night – I can't imagine anyone being very comfortable in the tombs that I saw!

no tourists in this picture

---

2   Operation 'Battle Axe' – a British attempt to halt the German siege of Tobruk – was planned for 15-17th June

One Year since Signing Up
15-06-41

Thank you all very much for the cables, they were well in time [*he was 21 on the 13th June, one year from signing up on his birthday in 1940*]. The day of days was the same as all the days here, we get the best out of every day and so our minor celebrations were not outstanding. I have just finished the airgraph letter and am sending the snap as promised. (*see picture section*)

It shows Percy on the left looking big and husky and horribly miserable (he was just leaving to go on his posting), Bill, centre, had just risen from his bed and I had just returned from a shower and I hadn't tucked my shirt in. However it gives the right ideas. Incidentally I'm half an inch taller than either of the others so the camera wasn't tilted in my favour. Also, I'm the only one that is correctly dressed (If only that shirt was tucked in!) The other two are wearing shoes but no belts.

with room-mates in Egypt, 1941

JULY '41

Trade tests and reunions
13-07-41

Quite a number of things have happened since I last wrote. Bill has been in and out of hospital – he had sand fly fever – the illness was short and sweet there are no flies on him now! In any case he was in a luxurious hospital, the nurses were Scottish, and he comes from Glasgow – what more could he want

Next, I have passed a trade test which makes me a Class II clerk; that mean another 6d a day and 1 years' service yet another 3d so I'm not doing too badly – although I have not seen either yet!

Several of the Aldershot boys have turned up on leave and we have swapped some lurid stories. Also, the lads who were with me in the training company at Clayton [*Clayton Barracks, Yorkshire*] were split up all over the Middle East and I have met several of them here. Stories of sand, stripes and new countries are inter-changed and then we part hoping to meet up in England.

And pictures too

Just recently I have been doing some gallant work with my camera – I think I told you that I had bought one. Well Bill and I have managed to snap each other at the top of the Pyramid – looking rather windblown (there's often quite a gale up there). There are others – I've got hopes of some good result so it will give you an idea of what this country looks like.

AUGUST '41

Dreams of things to come!
7-08-41

I met Ted [*Loughton – an acquaintance from Walthamstow*] last night for the first time. He is stationed outside Cairo and I introduced him to the 'Victory' and we had a good chat.

He says he has booked his passage back on a Wellington but I, myself would rather finish this business with a world tour – having come so far I wonder if the Army would send me back via India, China and USA – i would suit me fine, providing I knew home was at the other end.

Happy as a Private!

I don't believe I have ever mentioned my workmates; they are worth mentioning because we are a happy little band, remarkably efficient (true enough!) and if we go on at our present rate, we'll soon have this war finished.

In charge is 'The General' (three stripes); next 'The Harrier' whose nickname is obvious, but he also gets called 'Jock, Angus or Ivy '(the latter because he sticks to the wall when we walk home). He is 'Deputy General' and has one stripe, and the other two of us are really private privates upon whom the whole of S and T depends (Smithson, commonly known as Smithers and me – just commonly known!)

Providing we stick as we are, we will never have a stripe, we will cheer up everybody who enters our little department, and we will be home by this time next year![3]

Picture of Locals
14-08-41

I have taken quite a number of photos, some, of the Egyptian boys who are always asking for money etc, so you will be able to see for yourself what sort of people we mix with.

Many of the men wear a sort of frock that reaches the ground and have on their head either a fez or a kind of turban, while most of the women wear black clothes.

The children wear almost anything and as long as most of their body is covered, they don't seem to worry – in any case most of them go round bare foot.

---

3   Wishful thinking once again!

own pictures of locals

Busy times

The last few weeks stand out only for the things I have not done – No cinemas, no books, no leave. Never-the-less, I, and my pals have made up for this in other directions.

When we finish work we usually go to supper – bully or an 'Army' stew and then go for a stroll along the banks of the Nile, finishing up with an ice in the 'Victory'. The ice cream is our one daily luxury and seems to mix with anything previously eaten – anyway, we are all thriving.

SEPTEMBER '41
2-09-41

Local Friends

I had my day off about a week ago, spending the morning swimming (now with much effort I go forward instead of down) and in the afternoon met and chummed up with two more Egyptians.

They are students at one of the secondary schools here, at present on a 4-month vacation and are studying hard to enter the Cairo University. I have been out with them twice since and have met six others – all students.

One is a champion Boxer, and all speak excellent French and understandable English. I seem to have been 'adopted', firstly as a pal, secondly as an 'English Teacher' (one chap has threatened to bring his young brother along to hear English spoken 'properly')!

It's a great advantage knowing them because as we go about together, they point out and describe all sorts of things that I would normally miss.

Bazaars

Another new and interesting experience was a visit to the Bazaars. In narrow little alleys, just off the main streets, men were losing their eyesight making jewellery, engraving, fashioning beads and mosaic work.

In the dull light they had their noses almost on top of their work and to see the intricacy of the designs upon which they worked was in itself astonishing. That said, I will now always have a doubt of jewellery etc. after seeing glass, faced, polished and set-in rings and 'amber' beads, turned up on a lathe!

While these chaps worked others sold their wares – but not as in England. It took an hour and a half to buy some articles in one 'shop' and eventually we paid one quarter of the original price – I guess the vendor still makes a profit.

Once again smells were prevalent, real oriental perfumes were mixed with odours from queer foods, fruits, dogs and asses. Still as we didn't want Eastern slippers, brass dinner gongs, mother of pearl and imitation ivory bread boards etc we went as we came – quickly!

The Nile
12-9-41
I have sent you some pictures of the Nile, not far from where I live – it is ever so wide, nearly 1/2 mile at the island in the picture.

with bikes.' at the side of the Nile

Not so hot now

It is not so hot now – in fact the nights are cold, and we have to 'cover up' carefully. The cinemas without any roofs shut during the winter because of the cold and ordinary ones, like ours, open – a topsy turvy country!

Not mentioned in the letters but it is worth putting in that there was a German air raid on Cairo on 18th September in which 39 Egyptian civilians are killed and 100 injured, bringing condemnation against the Axis from the Arab and Muslim press.

OCTOBER '41

A home address at Last
3-10-41

Having received your 'airgraph' 7/9, I no longer consider myself an orphan of the storm etc – I now have a real home address to write to! [*you may remember that the family home had been bombed early on in the Blitz, Sept/Oct '40*].

I will have been on leave by the time this arrives but at present the one thing that I'm looking forward to is a bed! The last time I slept in a bed was on embarkation leave . Since then, I've slept on decks, sand, marble balconies, floors and tables, in trains, hammocks and armchairs, but never a bed!

Ramadan
7-10-41

The present month here is called Ramadan and all of the Mohammedans are fasting; they must not eat, drink or smoke from 8am to 6pm, so they sleep most of the day and have a very big meal at 2 am in the morning. I'm glad we do not have to – you should see them at our teatime – I bet they feel hungry!

Not the leave expected
18-10-41

I have been on leave – the leave itself was wonderful and I have rarely felt better- but wherever you might have imagined I was last week – I wasn't!

Leave to the place of my choice had been cancelled at the last moment. I had got to the station when I found that out, so some rapid planning was necessary which resulted in a trip of three days to Luxor and the rest of the time spent seeing the outlying sights of the big city – and have we seen some sights!

I travelled nearly 1000 miles in a week. Luxor was the chief city in Upper Egypt about 3000 years ago – it is mostly ruins but there are still many high buildings and wonderful statues standing and you will be able to see them in some of the pictures that I have sent.

The next two days were really fun. Food, bed, temples, ancient fords, mummies, sailing boats on the Nile, Korans, tombs and beer were all mixed up in a glorious whirl. Then it was back to Cairo by 7 am Thursday for another full day and if Thursday was a full day, Friday excelled it.

We rose before the larks – they call them kites out here- were at the station at 8.15 and after ½ hours journey transferred to donkey to visit more bits of ancient Egypt.

Five miles there and five miles back with a tour in between – I was sitting on that Donkey for about four hours. Ooooooh!

That was yesterday -today I'm realising it! I guess I will always remember my first leave in the East!

playing tourist in Luxor

NOVEMBER '41

In hospital
6-11-41
In the words of a better man than I 'I've been and gone and done it thi
time'. I've been sent to hospital, a slight touch of dysentery. However, the
disadvantage is offset by the beds, the care and the thought of food to come
I'll be back at work by the time you receive this – or, as I'm hoping, having
another spot of rest at the convalescent depot.

Trouble with local police
We have had some hectic times with our Egyptian pals. Once we were stopped
by our MPs [*Military Police*] and after vouching for them were OK'd and le
go – but when an Egyptian policeman threatened to take Fouad to prison a
a fifth columnist, it took us all our time to explain that we had known him fo
months and eventually we chased the policeman up the street!

It was good fun while it lasted but he dived down a dark alley so we left i
at that – could you imagine a thing like that happening in England!

Finally, while we were out together last week, we witnessed an accident -
a lorry knocked a donkey cart over. We went to assist but only by a piece o
luck escaped being involved in another. As we were lifting the cart anothe
lorry came along and hit it again – we shifted just in time. Spice of Life!!

Winter arrives + good results!
23-11- 41
Winter has arrived here, that is to say we have donned battle dress and shiver when we get under a cold shower, apart from that the weather is much like that in England say about June – cloudy but no rain.

Anyway, we are now seeing some results for the last few months of sweat and hard work so everyone is exceedingly bright and cheerful – we are to have a day off a week again which pleases everybody.[4]

More practice at bazaars
This afternoon I spent alone at the bazaars – they are as interesting as ever. As soon as you approach within a mile of them, locals of all ages and colours wearing multi-coloured clothes offer to show you round – commission men!

They take you to their own stalls – incidentally we are all 'Georges' or 'Johnies' to them and they are all 'Ahmed' or 'Ismahs' to us.

I got this afternoon's bargaining over pretty quickly, spending 1–2 hours at two shops – but to do this I had to convince them I was an old hand and walked away from each shop three times before I got the goods at my price. It's going to be strange to pay the price asked for when I'm back in England!

My day off hasn't finished yet (I'm in the Victory Club) so I'm off to read myself to sleep before the final tea and cakes – what a life – but it is only one day a week.

DECEMBER '41

Christmas Greetings from ME HQ
Copies of the Christmas Greeting cards sent are included in the Appendix. They were posted In October / November to arrive in good time for Christmas.

---

4   There were two good things going on at this time. The first – 'Operation Crusader' had started on 18th November and would end on 9th December with Rommel abandoning his 'Siege on Tobruk 'and withdrawing to Gazala. A major Allied success. The second, The Battle of Gondar, in Ethiopia (also covered by ME HQ) was the last stand of the Italian Forces in East Africa and was another significant result for the Allies. Such things evidently helped morale back at HQ.

The Daily Routine
12-12-41
I couldn't get everything on yesterday's airgraph so here's another dose. Our normal routine at present goes like this:

Awakened at 6 am by a clanging of bells (local reveille), on parade at 7.15 and go to work when it's over. This starts with 'office dusting' [*getting rid of the sand*], oil store filling, reading paper to get the news then work at 8.15.

Dinner at 12.15, back at 1.15 to oversee the locals cleaning the offices. (This happens every day, but we oversee it in a rota.) This should finish by 3 pm, then tea and back to work from 5– 8.15 – supper – then picquet [*watch duty – again on a rota*]. A grand life if you don't weaken but of course we rarely get so many of the 'odd jobs' done in one day – but it is good to get them done in one go.

Confined to barracks!
19-12-41
On Sunday a new NAAFI canteen opened in our billet and that combined with a heavy shower of rain (even that is news) made a wet night both inside and out. The new place is big and comfortable and will be quite pleasant when the novelty wears off and the crowd gets less. On Monday night it proved my undoing!

After a wet day – that has finished the rain for this year – I went into the Canteen after supper and with one or two of the other lads just sat and talked – a favourite pastime – but no drinks.

After the place closed, we went straight to bed and next morning I discovered that I had left my rifle in the police post all night and that I was well and truly 'on the peg' – result 4 days C.B., which makes me a fully initiated soldier! It at least gives me a chance to sew all the missing buttons on and maybe have some early nights!

The early hours are necessary too, for we have just had another hour a day tacked on, starting at 4pm every afternoon (54 working hours without any of the odd duties added). We are also having a two-day complete blackout practice which has resulted in screening the lamps as well as the windows – although I haven't heard any new words, I have heard some of the 'better' old ones often repeated as the lads collide in the dark!

A tank transporter for Christmas!
27-12-41

Last Wednesday (Christmas Eve*)*], the two offices of our branch had a dinner party! I assure you that it was a super success and none of us are quite sure what time it was that we saw each other home. As some chaps we saw couldn't have possibly got anywhere, let alone to their billet, I think we must have enjoyed ourselves.

We had to work on Christmas day until 12 noon when we finished for the day and would you believe, stuck right in the middle of one of the car parks was a huge tank transporter lorry with a German tank on board bearing the words **'A Christmas Present from the 8th Army'**

It was more than a present, it was an education[5] for that is the sort of thing that I have to work on, and I had never actually seen a transporter before, so I now know what I'm talking about!

Christmas Dinner was all that could be desired (from the Army) – the C in C came in and got the speech making over quickly – incidentally creating the impression of being a 'tough guy' – just the man, in fact. We took things steady after that lot and spent the evening at the 'Victory' where there was another party followed by a concert.

Boxing Day
26-12-41

Today is Boxing Day, but unlike all the previous ones I have had to spend this one at work – and I suppose most of the people in England have had to do the same. However, we have had a jolly good time and hope that you had the same.

It is worth adding another note here to point out that front line activity did not decrease over the Christmas period. Benghazi was recaptured by the British on 24th December and in a counter move Rommel inflicted many losses on British tanks on 27th enabling him to retreat and regroup. By 29th January Benghazi changed hands once again.

---

5   The 'education' into tank transport evidently paid off. It was to be instrumental in Dad later being successful in his application for a commission in the Indian Army and heading convoys both in India and in Burma.

JAN '42

A Year Since Leaving Barry
3-01-42

It is just a year today (Saturday) that I left Barry – and surprisingly enough, it is just as cold. Overcoats and gloves are the order of the day and most of the Egyptians are swathed in scarves and shawls.

After a joyful Christmas we reformed and went to Church last Monday – a concert, plus free tea and cakes and carol singing. It surprised us the fun we had letting ourselves burst forth into song and they could not give us enough – my pal made a nasty wise-crack, saying I sing very well on one note – so he has no trouble in harmonising. What a pal! What a voice!

Local Sandstorms
17-1-42

Sandstorms – you might like to know about them. I hope you are never in one. Not so bad in the city – but outside I know only too well, and my sympathy is with everyone out in the wide-open spaces.

From indoors it looks like a thin London 'pea-souper', a yellowish haze that all the car lights reflect on. From outdoors you don't really look at all, just feel a strong wind and yourself gradually getting dirtier and dirtier, eyes, ears and hair seem to get clogged and you feel as though you will not be clean for weeks. In 'the blue' [*the term for the Egyptian Desert*] it comes in swirls, in clouds or it just comes – a howling wind and the sand stings like the dickens and apart from feeling like you will not be clean for weeks – you aren't!

Time for a new posting?
24-1-42

I put in for a transfer to another branch the other day (the chance of becoming a sergeant appealed) but received the reply 'his services are being utilized to the best advantage in his present clerical capacity …. and it is not allowed to let him go.'

I ask you! Still, I might have ended up in the Far East or somewhere so I must stick around here for a bit longer 'In my present capacity' at no advantage to me!

This was not the only job application that Dad made at this time. He also applied to an advert for 'High Grade Cipher Personal' and mention in the letters is also made of his attempt to join 'the long-range penetration group' that was a result of Wingate's previous success with the Chindits. I for one am pleased that these particular attempts to find 'a new challenge' were not successful.

FEBRUARY '42

More pressure at Work
7-2-42 and 14-2-42

Work doesn't bear mentioning, as we are still pushed to the utmost – where we had thousands of vehicles, we now have millions, where we had long office hours we have longer.

My own news this week is really personal – I've just started on my third pay book and fifth pair of boots since receiving a number instead of a name and I've shifted my digs. Neither the bed space nor the boots are broken in yet but I'm hoping the pay book will be my last![6]

MARCH '42

I'm leaving here!
14/3/42

Here is the cream of the news – I'M LEAVING HERE. S'easy! Just as calmly and as collectively as that. This is the story:

A month ago, I applied (voluntarily) for a commission in the R.I.A.S.C; a fortnight later I was interviewed and passed; two days ago, I was interviewed again (both times by Lt Colonels) and passed again.

I am now awaiting events – although nothing is planned as yet, I think I am to go to OCTU [*Officer Cadet Training Unit*] in Bombay, do stacks of training there, then go to school and learn about everything and then, by the grace of Buddha, collect a pip! (sorry – star) – lucky Indians – Lucky Me!!

All I want from you is your blessing, good wishes and no worries because I worked it all out by myself and mean to see the job through properly. OK?

It may take weeks or months before anything happens. Put the flags out!!

---

5   Whilst telling those at home that he wanted to be back soon, it's clear that in reality he was more intent on a change of role. On 22nd February he applied for 'An Emergency Commission in the RIASC'. That is the Royal Indian Army Service Corp. As you will read shortly – this was successful!

APRIL '42

A Week to go – and promoted.
3-4-42

Sometime next week I leave here for the Base and from there I take the boat
note too that I have a 'tape' up [*i.e., promoted to Lance Corporal*] – I lose i
again when I reach the base, but it does not matter much as I receive sergeant
pay from the time I embark!

What with leaving and putting a 'stripe' up this week I have been receiving
congratulations from far and wide. Nevertheless, it was only the select few whc
celebrated and even then, you would <u>almost</u> say we did things moderately. A
the same, I haven't left yet and there may be more to come.

The next day or two is going to be fully occupied in buying necessities anc
throwing away lots of junk that seem to have accumulated so that I can close
my kitbag. At present it is a terrible weight being full of tins, bottles, spare
clothing, books and everything else required to bring joy and comfort to me

Quite a lot will have to go 'by the board' to make room for a battledres.
and two blankets!

One of 25 recruits
12-4-42

L/Cpl D Townsend
No, I Coy, RASC, Base Depot

As you will see from the above address I'm out of Cairo for the last time and a
present we are waiting for the boat. I have been here 4 or 5 days, thoroughly
settled in, been marching squads around, got brown all over again (surprising
how months of office work had 'paled' me) and met my new buddies for this trip

As usual – I'm the youngest (I have been everywhere so far) – but two
of the 25 are ex-Clayton Barracks and another comes from the old town
of Walthamstow!

I'm well away I assure you; all we will want when we parade our elephant:
around the houses will be 'Guardian' headlines of 'local boys make good'. In
fact, you better get them to set the type ready for the occasion for we do no
mean to be too long.[7]

---

7   Three and a half years was perhaps a little longer than expected – but that is what was in store!

Next letter in May is from Dehra Dun, India – in part 2!!

So the story continues in Part 2 which covers Dad's Officer training in the Indian Army, specialist Supplies and Motor Transport training, convoys across India and more besides. It will continue through the many months of battle at Imphal and the work needed to prepare for the move south into Burma and on to victory in August '45.

Whilst this is happening, the East Africa Campaign continued. Heavy losses were inflicted on British armoured divisions by Axis on 'Black Saturday' – 13th June 1942, just two months after Dad had left for Bombay. Axis captured Tobruk on 21st June and by 30th June the Axis forces reached El Alamein and attacked the Allied defences. The first battle of El Alamein had begun.

The first battle of El Alamein was not a success for the Allies:

The 8th Army launched a series of attacks as Axis dug in but by 31st July, Auchinleck, the Allies Commander, called off the offensive. Churchill was not pleased and showed it by dismissing Auchinleck and replacing him with Bernard Montgomery as Field Marshal and Head of the 8th Army on 13th August.

Interestingly, given how successful Montgomery was to become, he was not Churchill's first choice. Lt General William Gott, the first choice, was killed on his way to assume command. Montgomery proceeded to become one of the most famous of war time heroes, leading the allies to victory in the second battle of El Alamein between 23rd October and 5th November 1942.

After their defeat in the second battle of El Alamein, the remnants of Rommel's Afrika Korps were forced into Tunisia. In a new initiative by the Allies, 'Operation Torch', a considerable number of Anglo-American landings were made in North-West Africa in November '42. After numerous battles against 'Vichy France' forces (who then changed sides) the Allies encircled several hundred thousand German and Italian personnel in North Tunisia and finally forced surrender in May 1943.

That part of the war was over. Greater battles were now to take place in India and in Burma where a young man who was not yet 22 was to be very much involved.

PART 2

Preparing for Battle

May 1942 – November 1943

Officer Cadet D.A. Townsend, Dehra Dun, India, 1942

CHAPTER 6

The War in Asia up to 1942

Whilst the Italians had been Germany's prime collaborators in the Western Desert Campaign in North Africa, it was the Japanese who were the main adversaries of the Allies in Asia.

Japan had gone to war against China in 1937 with the intent of becoming the dominant force in the Asia Pacific. They believed that the tripartite agreement signed with Germany and Italy in September 1940, would help them realise their ambition. Initially this proved to be very much the case and there were plenty of early successes.

Japan bombed Pearl Harbour on 7th December '41 and this was quickly followed by co-ordinated attacks on American bases in the Philippines, Guam and Wake Islands. Hong Kong also fell in December, Singapore in February '42 and much of Malaysia was over-run shortly thereafter.

Japan's success was largely due to them defying the 'Colonial view' of how a war should be waged and this was to be more evident in Burma than anywhere else.

Quoting from E D Smith's excellent 'Battle for Burma':

"Without being deliberately racist, it was genuinely believed that one white soldier was more than capable of seeing off two or three coloured ones. How then, they asked, could these little men with prominent teeth, peering myopically through thick glasses, thrash British soldiers in battle after battle, culminating in the ignominious scuttle from Burma in 1942."

Fall of Burma 1942

Burma had been under British rule since 1824 and the concept that war could be waged in the jungles of Burma was unthinkable to those in command.

Reality was very different. The Japanese did not regard the jungles of Burma as a significant barrier to a successful outcome. They went through Burma with victory after victory. They adjusted to jungle warfare whereas the Allies did not. The direct result was that British forces were compelled to make the biggest retreat that had ever taken place, covering 900 miles in four months and costing more than 13,000 British and Indian casualties. Japanese casualties of 4500 were modest by comparison.

By the middle of 1942 there were no longer any Allied troops left on Burmese soil. The retreat had gone from Rangoon and Mandalay in the south right back to India in the north. The one singular exception was a comparatively small corner in the north, which was inhabited by Chinese.

It was a huge success for Japan and a huge loss for the Allies. Significant rebuilding and retraining of Allied forces was now required.

Next step India!

The Allies knew that Japan's next intent was to invade India and take advantage of the unrest that Gandhi and his fellow congress leaders were stirring up. It would be a logical and very significant target. If allowed to succeed it would dramatically change the course of the war.

Dad's recruitment into the Indian Army in May '42 along with many other British officers, had been as a direct consequence of the Burma retreat that had started earlier that year.

The supplies and transport training that he had been recruited for, was a key requirement both for the initial battle and for the major part that tanks were expected to play later on. Significant forces were also trained in jungle warfare which, to date, had been a weakness from an Allied perspective.

The Indian Army was increased overall from 200,000 in 1939 to 2.5 million by August 1945 and India played a huge role in assisting the Allies on three continents as well as safeguarding its own borders.

The Japanese believed the best route into India was either through the eastern seaboard of Arakan or via the mountain routes of Imphal and Kohima in the state of Manipur. These were to be the sites of the battles to come and were all on Indian soil. Only by being successful in these could the Allies work south to retake Burma.

But let us not get ahead of ourselves. First a good deal of training was in order.

CHAPTER 7

The Sandhurst of India

May – August 1942

MAY 1942

[from his extended letter to Connie Pead in April 1945.]

Sailing from Cairo was different to sailing from Liverpool in January '41. Just two weeks rather than ten – and the fish are more interesting! Schools of porpoises do their tricks daily and flying fish seemed to be holding long distance manoeuvres with flights up to a hundred yards. Two ports of call and Urdu to study filled in the time – but I would be glad to see land again.

I had time to think things over a bit and decided that my stay in Egypt wasn't too bad, but I definitely didn't wish to return for a long, long time.

Arrival in India

We spent a pleasant day and a half in Bombay, liking it very much after our journeyings. It is much more colourful than Egypt, for even the poorer people favour a splash of colour. You see vivid red railway porters, blue and yellow policemen, multi coloured saris etc.

It was a change too, to see normal double-decker buses and big trams, not ramshackle things of old; and what we found most sensible – fans everywhere – which took all the discomfort out of the heat.

During our wanderings we were impressed by the splendour of the buildings and approached one that appeared to be a cross between a church and the Houses of Parliament – it was one of the railway termini!

We entered – almost in deference – into a huge marble pillared hall, very much like the interior of a mosque, passed through a door and stepped into – WATERLOO!!

It was the exact replica – and we found it somewhat staggering. A little tact and chatting and we were shown over the electric engine which tows the Poona Express – a very good introduction to India!

We left Bombay at night, 3rd class with wooden seats and the journey took 40 hrs – two nights, sleeping on board. We used our own bedding and I kipped about six feet from the floor on a bunk 15 inches wide – it says something for Army training that I did not role off!

Bombay to Dehra Dun (Himalayan foothills!)

The journey included every type of country from mountains to rolling plains, forests to deserts, grass land to dusty bush country. Most of the rivers were dry, awaiting the monsoon which starts in June but the green trees and near Dehra Dun, the grass, looked the 'goods' to us.

To give you an idea of distance – Bombay to Dehra Dun is about the same as London to Rome!

We passed through Delhi and came up into these hills; it is two thousand feet up here, very hot but, as I say, like England. About 6 miles away, as the crow flies, is a hill station, 7000' up – i.e., 5000' above us, and it is 22 miles by road – with many a precipice thrown in. I'm told that one of our first tests is to get there and back (not using the road) in a day. A good job we had some practice climbing!

The Sandhurst of India
13-5-42

Here is the long since promised letter with all my news. First the new address, although by the time the letter arrives, I may have left again for I should only be here for three or four months:

OFFICER CADET D.A. Townsend, British Wing, IMA (India Military Academy), New Forest, DEHRA DUN, United Provinces, India.

It is recognised as the Sandhurst of India and is located north of Delhi, in the foothills of the Himalayas – and what a change it is from Cairo!

Our new surroundings are almost too much like those of England to be comfortable; the same countryside, lush with plenty of trees (not palms!) plenty of birds that aren't like Egypt's kites and crows; wonderful accommodation (our wing is in tents attached to the academy proper), two in a tent (I was in a tent with 15 others a month ago!) bed, furniture, share of servant, super food, early to bed and early to rise. That is the situation in a nutshell, who could complain?

By the time I've finished this course I should be useful as an officer in any arm of the service. We are taught driving, signalling, Urdu, administration, drills, and everything else, with plenty of PT and exercises and other stunts; in fact, the first 2 mile run last night has left me as stiff as a board – tonight's should loosen me up again – I hope!

So much for this place for the present; my immediate worry is in spending a £35[8] clothing allowance to the best advantage – the first step to 'an officer and a gentleman'.

I have just remembered! I began to grow a moustache while on the boat, mainly as an experiment to fill the time… it looks as though it is going to be a good one, so I will keep you informed as to progress!

Finally, just for your information, the cash situation is fine this end. I'm on sergeants pay (6/6 per day), keep, barber, bearer included, and we work on a credit system whereby we sign chits for everything and collect the balance about once a month – a system that is going to require a good 'settling down to'.

'all smiles before training starts'

---

8   The level of pay – £120 pa – puts the £35 clothing allowance in perspective – they wanted their future officers to be well dressed!

Two weeks in
26-5-42 and 10-6-42
Well, I've now been here just over a fortnight, really settled down and we begin work in earnest in a day or two… I like the place and the life, so I feel that you should know all about everything.

A choice piece of English countryside surrounded by mountains puts the situation in a nutshell; it is lovely after the sand, all flowers and trees, beautiful birds and butterflies and a wonderful assortment of insect life. The insects make quite an impression (in more ways than one). We've simply got everything – spiders, ants up to half an inch, caterpillars, fireflies (very nice at night), beetles, mosquitoes, grasshoppers and crickets, ordinary and a few local varieties too.

The weather is bearable, hotter than England but so far, much cooler than Egypt. The best bit is that it rains about twice a week and continues with colossal electric storms. More rain fell in the first half hour than I had seen since I left England! Incidentally there is so much lightning that it is easier to count the periods of darkness in between!

The normal routine
In spite of having bearers to do the normal 'housework' i.e., boot-cleaning, bed-making, water carrying etc, our life is not one of ease. I'm wakened at 5 am, expected to be on parade at 5.50 and until 8.15 am bashed around a field being taught the Indian methods of rifle drill and so on.

Then comes breakfast and from 9.15 to 1.30 we simply soak up everything that comes our way – lessons of every kind. Afternoons are free until 4.30 (a slight snag develops as we have to clean rifles on alternate afternoons) and then for an hour we have what are called 'Olympics'.

Perhaps the name speaks for itself but if it does not then I'll tell you that we 'indulge' in. PT, hockey, football, cross country runs, boxing and unarmed combat (the easiest methods of killing people with the bare hands) – in fact, everything that I'm not used to!

Bath and more notes at 6pm. From 7–8 each night we are having private Urdu lessons, then comes dinner proper – 8 courses on any restaurant menu – soup, fish, dinner, sweet, savoury, coffee, cheese and biscuits, dessert – every night! I'm only too pleased to crawl into bed immediately after dinner, i.e., at 9pm – Happy Days!!

'8 courses on any restaurant menu'

And then that bit extra

This is roughly the normal procedure when we are 'at home' but to add a little spice to life we go out on exercises regularly and study tactics and general organisation.

So far, we have had only one of these jaunts, but many are promised. This one lasted two days, the night being spent sleeping in the jungle (until the thunderstorm broke in the early hours) and it was here that I had a shake up with a jackal – but survived!

How old?

I've just realised that I'm 22 in a day or two – I feel like 72, the Army has put years on me, but I guess a good night's sleep will bring me back to normal! NB. The moustache is doing well!

Though things are winding up, the work hasn't changed much, still plenty of PT, night exercises and things like 'Water Buffalo' thrown in! I didn't seem to stop from 5 am last Monday morning until 1.30 pm yesterday (Saturday).

One exercise that might interest you was a compass march – a map, a compass and a jungle seem to be the only requirements, but a suit of armour is recommended.

We had to cover a mile and it looked fairly easy on the map but on the ground, it happened to contain three ravines with almost sheer sides and no human foot had ever set foot where we went. Dense under growth with every plant containing a difficult type of thorn and we had to go almost direct!

My pal took a step forward and went into a ten-foot hole; we both went bottom first into a stream when our hand hold broke as we were descending a thirty foot canyon – we came out within twenty yards of our objective and were then told to find our way back!!

All carried on for 4 months as planned – Officer Cadet D Townsend became 2ⁿᵈ Lt Townsend, successfully passing out of the IMA on 28ᵗʰ August 1942.

with other successful lieutenants , August '42

'first pip received'

CHAPTER 8

Specialist Training and Christmas in Kashmir

September '42 – January '43

SUPPLIES COURSE
30-9-42

2nd LT D.A. Townsend 'B' Co RIASC School, Kakul, NWFP, India

The first long letter from another 'home'. First, I'll re-assure you (as if it was necessary) that I'm fine and hope that you all are. This is going to be a colossal story as you will see from the number of pages – I suggest you all seat yourselves comfortably round the fire and have Shirley [*Dad's sister*] read it to you.

The story: first the place, then how I got here; what I mean to do whilst here and then a few other bits and pieces too!

The place

I'm now in **Kakul**. You won't find it on a map but it is very close to (and above) Abbottabad which you will see in the north west corner of any map of India; it's in the NW Frontier Province [*now part of Pakistan*] in the foothills of the Himalayas just 200 miles south of Russia. An open valley 4200' up, completely surrounded by mountains, with snow-capped peaks in the distance; a walk in any direction means a hard climb up or down once you leave the road – that is 'home' for the next few months.

I'm now actually closer to Kabul in Afghanistan than I am to Bombay!

Where I live the valley begins to slope upwards towards the hills, giving me a view right down the valley, looking on the top of the nearest town, four miles away – generally covered in a thin mist when I first look out in the morning.

By the time you receive this it is quite possible that the whole scene will be covered in snow – I'll forward my comments later!

How I got here and what I mean to do

Having finished at Dehra Dun I was posted to 'Supplies' at Jhansi. I was only there for two weeks and then they sent me here. But it was long enough to know that I don't want to go back. Inevitable at some stage I guess – but I'm in no rush!

Now I am here I have once again to go to school. To learn everything about SUPPLIES and the RIASC [*Royal India Army Service Corp*] from baking bread, judging cattle, from motor lorries to camel transport. I'll be busy don't worry!

This course is then followed by another one also based here on Motor Transport. This will include lots of driving on the mountain roads and knowing motors inside out. Learning how to collect wrecks from the beds of rivers and to repair them afterwards. It's going to be so much more interesting than the footslogging of Dehra Dun!

After this I hope to use this knowledge further East and then whistle back home to see you all.[9]

Three months were spent in 'Supplies' training – more is said in the letters home about the climbing adventures on Sundays, the one day off they had, than about the course itself. As an example:

Days off!

Now for it – here is the epic, the story of how three brave (?) men spend their Sundays in between piles and piles of work. – Climbing Up hills and down again.

Each week is the same except a different spot of Mountain is used; sometimes the weekly official free-for-all route-march cum mountain climb follows the same course – in that case we know the route and take the easiest course knocking off corners with the greatest of ease. However, we never let this mid-week hike deter us from the Sunday special, so off we go.

…. *A long description follows and then* … You will have to imagine the climb, for although we stopped long and often no snaps were taken. because we had to hold on! At long last we arrived.

……I leave you to imagine how we all sleep on Sunday nights – and how we dash back to the fray on Monday mornings. What we do until the next

---

9   The reality was he did not come back until 1946 but interesting that he was planning a return much earlier!

weekend is taboo but the whole life is healthy, interesting, enjoyable and fast moving – the weeks are rushing past and that is all I ask; no boredom.

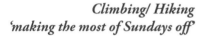

Climbing/ Hiking
'making the most of Sundays off'

The 'Supplies' course was successfully completed. He then stayed at the same location to do his 'Mechanical Transport' course – but it was almost Christmas and a very special trip had been planned:

CHRISTMAS IN KASHMIR - DECEMBER 1942

RIASC School, KAKUL, N.W.E.P.
30-12-42

Motor Coach, 'All aboard for Kashmir'

Here is the story you have been waiting for, the 'travels in wonderland', but before I start let me first hope you are all in good health and are keeping well occupied in your various duties and pastimes . You are all ok, good. Lets' go.

I gave you a rough idea of our plans by the normal mail; how George first had the idea, how we wrote to houseboat agents, motor companies and the police , sorted out the town for buses and got generally worked up. Well, everyone of those plans materialised, we chose our bus, easily gathered a party to fill it (most of the lads came with me from Middle East and Dehra Dun – George of course being the exception as he was not in Middle East), finally selected a hotel in preference to a house boat owing to extreme cold, and most amazing of all, our permit to use the road by night was presented to me in the form of a late telegram while I was sitting on 'our' bus waiting to move off. Actually when I returned here I received confirmation in writing 'on behalf of His Highnesses' Government', signed by the Home Secretary of Kashmir!

Our journey, or any journey on that road, should go down in history!

In all the distance was 160 miles from our camp to the hotel in Srinegar; about 100 of those were along a road cut out of the mountain face high above the river valley which we had to follow and the number of bends was absolutely uncountable – a stretch of straight 100 yards long was rare and at one point I counted thirty five bends (nothing less than a right angle) in five minutes as we ascended the mountain range and then gave it up as a bad job!

During the first fifty miles the bus had to be halted three times for various lads to lose their lunches and most of the others looked that way. I myself am always lucky in this matter and never feel any effects of violent hills and bends or altitude but I shall never pay to go on a switchback after this, knowing that one can get the same sensations on a public road – now perhaps you understand why it is closed after dark and we needed the special permit. For the best part it was typical mountain road, a rocky wall on one side sloping up to the pine and snow clad peaks, a big drop on the other side , generally varying from 50 to about 300 feet although in one spot there was a sheer drop of over a thousand feet.

At night we were stopped three times and only the telegram kept us going – silent prayer all round; the driver, who was a marvel, kept his foot down in spite of passing through rain and snow storms and delivered us safely at 9.30pm after being exactly eight hours on the road and having taken about a dozen stops.

We were definitely not expected! Our wine had arrived but the letter sent days before had not, so things were not completely prepared. Would we settle n and wait a few more minutes while dinner was prepared? Sure, we would do anything for food, so we made ourselves at home, opened our bottles and settled in as asked.

Before I go any further I want to warn you and apologise that this is a story of much food and drink – it is not quite fair to you but our leave came to consist of short rests between big meals of such exceptional quality that to return here was an immediate goal for all!

Anyway, this first dinner was announced as ready at about 11pm. Possibly a bit later, by which time we were primed and ready to eat anything, but the 'pot luck' feast with which we were presented set most of us back on our heels and left us gasping; five or six courses, any one of which would have been a meal in itself were placed before us and the discomforts of the journey were soon forgotten. Retiring to cosy little rooms holding one or two, all with blazing pine log fires ensured that the day would end in an appropriate manner – and it did!

One or two details need to be filled in – there were thirteen of us and the hotel was ours, no other guests being in existence, therefore we did what we liked. Originally our party had been fourteen but one unfortunate came a cropper at football the night before we set out (broken bones and one eye shut completely) and had to stay behind. The weather was bitterly cold but dry and by the help of eight thicknesses of blankets and our fire by night and all available clothing by day it was easily overcome. Now, to go on. Not bored I trust!

Naturally we didn't quite rise with the dawn but I was awakened by the bells of the Protestant church which was only a few yards down the road. Some consciences were pricked and a few of the lads turned to the service later on. I rose leisurely, glanced out of the window and had my first daylight view of yet another capital - a wide canal, crammed full of houseboats of all shapes and sizes, all looking rather bleak. Breakfast finished - I daren't go into details - and George and I began a tour of exploration.

The sun began to shine and emphasised a thing we had missed - snow mountains in every direction – Srinagar lies in a flat valley locked in by these mountains and has water everywhere – to call it Venice on ice will give you some idea. The river we had followed en route , the Jhelum, meanders round the valley, huge lakes cover acres and acres, canals go in every direction and lots of the native population reside in boats. All the roads that are not 'pukka' or metalled are inches deep in mud and people wear wooden clogs of large proportions , cloven like a cows hoof to prevent themselves sinking. One other strange thing was that nearly all of them were swathed in blankets and carried beneath these blankets , small wicker baskets containing earthenware pots of glowing charcoal embers – a most sensible idea which we took up rapidly causing amusement to everyone we met.

Having endeavoured to raise a new appetite we retired to the 'club', became temporary members and proceeded to further stimulate it – the vicar , the remainder of our party and most of the congregation all had the same idea so it must have been good – the club was rather crowded !

We had disposed of large portions of duck and sundry other items for lunch when a lady announced and proceeded to issue an invite to the multitude to take Xmas tea with her – the vicar's sermon had had its effect when she saw our poor, lonely contingent in church. The offer was graciously accepted and we filled the gap by a little more exercise combined with sight-seeing – ending up by driving our own tongas, almost to her door.

It seemed as if nothing could go wrong. We had been afraid that it would be an affair where we had to balance tea on one knee and make polite refusals with any spare limb not otherwise engaged, but it was not so. The hostess was a lady of 60 odd and was assisted by a younger woman, a German Jewess refugee and after they had sat us down to another spread of cakes ad lib, and filled us to the brim, admirably entertained us with music and songs. The old lady was excellent on the piano, so we returned a few efforts at community singing and the evening flew by. It filled a gap that may have lagged otherwise and everybody seemed the better for it. This evening I've written a short but touching note of thanks on behalf of the party , which should be well received – after all, I may go back one day !

A crowd of overfed individuals, we oozed rather than walked by the canals to our own hotel, to be greeted by a host of 'Kashmiri art dealers'. Kashmir shawls are world famous , the carved wood work, the paper mashie and silverware are equally so and unlike India, at least here there were crowds of them, not selling but politely offering to send boats or tongas the following morning to take us to their show places.

It sounded as good as anything so we accepted a couple of offers and turfed the lot out to settle down to dinner. As it was our own show we had it in style - George and I as the 'arrangers' had been out and spent plenty of cash on behalf of everyone – a dry martini cocktail to start with, white wine to help things along, sherry to finish up, oranges, lemons,gingers and ciders for the few TT's and had told the proprietor to add any extras to the feast and bill to make it fit for the gods. It was, but there were no extras on the bill and I regret to say that one or two had to miss the final course owing to sheer lack of space – the rest of us refused to be 'done' although it was touch and go and it was a true feeling of benevolence that we reached the end and toasted 'the missing ones'!

We were enjoying ourselves and decided that everybody else should too. We proceeded to the biggest and most famous hotel in town where there was a dance and a bar – two chaps even danced! It was a good place for our purpose but we were unanimous that it did not compare with our own for anything else – large, cold and bleak, twice as dear, with titles, retired double chins and fine examples of the English 'mem-sahiba' in her cups and plenty of the 'How daw yaw daw' language flying about, We left them rather more normal at 12.30pm and called it a day.

Boxing Day dawned – so I am told, it was well advanced when we took to the shikari boat which had come for us and were gently paddled down the river. That gave us Srinegar from a new angle , enabling us to see more of the house boats , the strange shaped barges with their owners living aboard, the rickety bridges and houses balanced over the water , the many mosques all with roofs made of sheet tin from petrol cans, the Maharajah's old palace and hosts of people in the strangest of costumes.

The arrival at the 'showroom' was in itself spectacular – the boat pulled up against a steep mud bank beneath a perilously perched erection - a plank was placed on the slope and we were expected to walk up. I needed a quite undignified push and even then didn't make the grade but ended up by almost pulling the building over in an effort to haul myself up - I can climb over 20 foot walls with the aid of a rope by struggling a lot but not up a plank 'no hands!' It was worth it though, for inside we were shown a wonderful display of work – all hand done, wood carving, embroidery and engraving , good materials of all colours; once again time flew and another meal had to be attended.

31/12

If only we had 48 hour days I might get some place with my letter writing – as it is now I'm miles behind with my notes and still have piles of letters to write. To continue:

Our presence in Srinagar had by this time become public news, every time we went back to the hotel we were greeted by showers of salesmen – I swear one spent the day on our doorstep (incidentally it was a nice feeling once again to have a door you could shut in someone's face) and we became adept at clearing the unwanted crowd.

Our numbers were slightly diminished as a few of the boys had gone to a near-by 'snow resort' and later returned after a day of skiing, sledging and photography – but we did not put up a bad show ourselves. The morning had been well spent, at lunch the proprietor slipped in and said "Please don't go out to tea today – I've something special arranged for you". After the previous efforts we felt we could not let him down, therefore more exercise was necessary. A hill rises sharply from the flat plain giving a splendid view of everything – we struggled up it during the afternoon and were well repaid. The view was stupendous , mountains all round with their crests popping up above the clouds , terrific lakes giving lovely reflections of the snows , the town laid out like a map just showing how much water there really was , the river giving a better corkscrew effect than any corkscrew could ever hope to and on the lakeside, the new palace looking like a model housing estate, added to which we found the blind side of the hill to be covered with snow, the old felt young again and all were happy !

The tea party was just as good as all the rest of the grub – another cake and lashings of extras was rounded off by the arrival of our absentees together with the dealer we had visited in the morning, with more wares for display. By the time we had seen, admired and moved him on it was almost dinner time - then , when that was over our day began !

Having become a member of 'the club' we started there, used up a few remaining coupons, prepared ourselves for the 'frost so cruel' and adjourned to the scene of the previous nights activities. This time the reception wasn't so frigid – not that we cared one iota. Seven of us formed a pool and used the table tennis table – after the sixth round of the evening I learned a form of the game that I never knew existed.

Between us we monopolised this and then got the crowd interested in 'our' form of darts – pinned a rupee note (4 inches by 2 inches) on the dart board , charged 4 annas a throw and the note went to the first dart piercing it. Easy? Possibly, but not when the crowd are slightly fuzzy - work it out , there are 16 annas in a rupee so we were giving fairly good odds but at the end we put Rs19 into our pool. It was thirsty work so we gave it up and then concentrated on the table tennis.

Then we found that George was missing, instituted a search and scoured the ground floor – not a room was missed. He walked in the main entrance

as I and another chap reached the first landing on the main stair! Last years'
lesson was remembered – no, mixing of drinks – so we were merrily three
parts gone but fit for anything. It had gone midnight and we decided it was
time to give it good , linked arms and made for home. Out the main gate,
turn left, so far so good – a voice from the distance. "Wait for me". George?
No another of the gang, not in the pool – he came straight across country
while we let 'Good King Wensleslass' ripple gently from our bosoms.

The straggler stopped, seemed to rise in the air, descended to earth and
came on – I remember looking at the chap nearest me, he was looking at me
but apparently we were both thinking the same thing for neither of us said
a word. The next morning I went back to the scene just to make sure I knew
I hadn't been that bad for on my return I had made the fire , attended to
George who was a slight casualty, done some packing, cleaned my teeth and
turned in – and there it was, an unbroken four foot fence right along the road
side, with two strands of barbed wire making it about five foot in all , our
straggler had come over that with ease but he couldn't remember a thing that
had happened after 11pm – a super night from beginning to end.

Very little could be done on the Sunday before we returned. The church
bells again woke us and a final look round the town followed by a round- up
of the gang and we were ready to move off. We had meant to leave at 12.30
but it was almost an hour later before we shifted – the driver went as one
possessed and took almost exactly seven hours to do the trip. He free wheeled
nearly one third of the way by coasting down every incline, and luckily for
us knew the road like a book, roaring into blind hairpin bends, slowing only
on one or two that experience must have taught him the necessity to do so.

In spite of so much food and drink not a soul was sick on the return trip. That
helped the speed and so did my quick work at the two toll gates and customs –
we had to be nippy because the worst of the road was nearer home and to take
it in the dark would have been risky if not suicide. We made it safe and sound ,
slept like logs and since then have been back to the normal routine with, as I said,
all my spare time spent in letter writing – this is the 28th page in four days !

On Tuesday I had my first go at driving any distance on roads, real twisty,
dangerous mountain roads in a three tonner – previously all time at the wheel
had been on special circuits. I enjoyed it immensely and am now ready for
anything from a scooter to a ten tonner!

That is about all, you will get the story again in pictures when they come
through. It is New Years Eve, a lousy night, cold and pouring with rain, the

tent is leaking in a few spots but the fire is going well so I'm going to turn in and leave it to the others to celebrate. I've had my good time. This being the last letter I will write this year I have just closed the account. 185 in 12 months, not a bad average and particularly good for the Post Office!

All very best wishes to you all – keep bright and hearty and maintain a steady flow of letters in this direction, they are always welcome and most of them seem to find me (two this week were each five months old) . I'm bound to be miles away from here when you receive this – that only means more journeys , new places and more to write about – you lucky people.

Arrival in Srinegar

soldiers in snow
'Boxing Day 1942'

Shikar boat - as used for taxi ride

JANUARY '43

MECHANICAL TRANSPORT COURSE

A typical week!
12-1-43
I'm going out on a night convoy in an hour's time which will put a sudden end to writing much.

This week has all been spent on the road – out all day Monday, pouring rain, bitterly cold, driving through clouds; all day Tuesday, snow and rain, but still going strong and enjoying the driving (we have vehicles which are open in the front, no windscreen at all, so if it rains and blows you know all about it!)

Today has been more ordinary from the work point of view and has been one of brilliant sunshine (such is the variety of our weather), tomorrow we are carrying troops and Friday will be out all day again driving across country. I'm due to leave here at the end of the month to go to an MTT unit (I hope) where I should constantly be 'on the road'.

15/1: interlude – I had to give up writing the other evening for our night trip – it went quite successfully and was good fun. Yesterday the little Ghurkhas were given a shake up in our wagons all according to plan and today has been simply superb. It has been a glorious day for the time of year, almost cloudless, bitterly cold and frosty to start with but quite warm later, especially as we were being energetic.

The outing was a trip of about 90 miles and included ten across country, through rivers and all sorts of impossible going – quite the sort of stuff we marched through at Dehra Dun but slightly easier with a motor to pull us along. I was driving a three tonner and didn't get stuck once, which isn't bad at all, but a lot of the time had to be spent in pushing and digging others out to clear the way and in some places we had to dig our own passage – break down river banks to climb out of the water and so on.

One thrill which I didn't take part in (much!!) was when going along a track hard against the bank on the right side and the ground under the left front wheel, being the edge of a ten foot drop, crumbled away. The lads got excited and in their various ways, pointed out our danger, so I put my foot down and got across just in time – that was only one of my 'little incidents'!

A thing we came up against several times was a sharp ascent between two high banks and a deep gully in the middle where the water drained away –

one wheel in the gully and you were sunk – the fact that the lorry was often at a hideous angle had been ignored, we had been given two places on the map and were following the only link between them – a canal track!

Now, on arrival back, we all decided it had been the best outing out to date – really good fun but it has left me dead tired after fighting with a jumping steering wheel for hours. Friend George and his crew were stoned by one set of villagers, but I and my gang made great use of the folks we met by asking the way and I had a small boy sitting on the spare wheel by my side pointing out the best roads – sorry tracks – between the fields, hedges and rivers, for the greater part of the journey.

He only led me astray once and then it was partly my fault. We had to cross a river with a steep bank on one side, and having done the easy bit I just couldn't go any further. I backed up and had another go but in vain, so finally decided to ooze along the edge of the river downstream until we found a small space to turn round and climb up at an angle. All's well that ends well!

Mobile Mechanics
23-1-43

They have set us various 'problems' with respect to recovering vehicles – or should I say 'wrecks'. Let me use a picture (*included in picture section*) to explain just one.

Now maybe it doesn't look difficult until you look carefully at the picture I had one of these to rescue with a party of five helpers. Try and imagine the slope, the chap holding the camera was standing at the top, the two you can see are at least level with the superstructure:- but that is not all. The lorry is resting against a small tree which you can't see, behind that is 'nothing' A cliff, almost sheer, drops away for 100' and you can see the bottom of the drop, in the right hand corner, with a couple of trees on the side of the cliff.

Believe me, you have to be gentle besides forceful, to bring these lorries back on 'dry land'.

In all we have collected nine so far; how they were put in such positions is more that I can guess – getting them back was quite difficult enough for us The vehicles are three tonners, big things and very much exposed in these days of wind and rain.

Here are a couple more pictures (*see picture section*) just to give you an idea of some of our other 'problems'.

As ever both of these were even more difficult than the pictures suggest

With the one on the left the vehicle was neatly jammed between the slopes and the lads were told to shift it without using equipment!

mobile mechanics in action

Later that month

It began to get colder and colder, the sun disappeared, the valley in which we lived was in clouds most of the time and it began to snow – the first I had seen (at least at close quarters) since 1939!

It used to snow and melt daily at first but the snowline on the mountains gradually came down until at last we sloshed around like Eskimos. Convoys on mountain roads covered in snow first taught me to drive properly – at least I thought I was doing fine until one of my pals put a wagon over the edge, killing everyone on board – then I revised my own capabilities!

Time to leave
23-01-43

I'm leaving here in a week from today on the 30th January and all I know at present is that I'm going to a unit in Delhi. I'm hoping that when I get there they will give me a further address and are just sending us there for security reasons. However, before joining this unit we are to have 10 days leave, which I mean to spend in Lahore. This city is the best I have seen in India as yet and happens to be en-route. Two good reasons for me making the visit.

So 2/LT (soon to be LT) Don is stepping out into a new life where he has sepoys of his own to look after and be their mother and father all in one! At present we are having a final batch of tactical schemes- I've been out all day today (Sat) and on Monday we are going out for two days non-stop, on a real war of our own making; actually I've landed the job of an umpire and will have to decide when and where other people go wrong and make suggestions for corrections when we hold an inquest on the affair. So will have to know my onions!

28-01-43

Today we've signed out and also received our reports – 'a capable and practical officer, works hard and is thorough, best suited to MT but would do well in any branch of the Corps'de da de da!!

The course was successfully completed without further significant incidents in February 1943.

Training Locations in India
© Sally Townsend

CHAPTER 9

First Postings and 'The Great Trek'

February – June 1943

FEBRUARY '43

Next New Address: B MTT Training Group, Kingsway, New Delhi
1-2-43

Our leave, spent in Lahore, finished yesterday. We arrived here, 3 miles from Old Delhi, nine miles from New Delhi with all our goods and chattels intact, reported, set up a home, engaged a new bearer, had some grub and went to bed.

That was yesterday: today we've turned out in shorts to combat the sun (glorious weather), saluted hundreds of over-enthusiastic sepoys, said how d'ye do to one or two of 'the best people' and generally made ourselves known.

As far as I can see we are going to be busy which is how we like it; but may go anywhere at any time in the future – things just rest in the lap of the gods i.e., GHQ who will put us where we are most needed.

At present there seems to be plenty of everything, vehicles, soldiers, work and food – I guess I'm going to like it here however long the stay.

Two weeks later – training new recruits
28.2.43

As for me, well I'm having a super time:

I'm attached to a company with 50 junglies who, two weeks ago were swinging from bough to bough [*not politically correct but times change!*] and I've to turn them into soldiers.

To be more exact they are straight from the fields, few of them have handled money and only 2 can write their names: yet we get along fine. Every morning I take them for a run and on return join in their PT, letting the naik (corporal) drill me with them – they are tickled to death with the idea and I've quickly got to know them all.

At present they are being taught to march – (painful, for it's the first time that most of them have worn boots), and also to read and write, with all the old essential instruction thrown in.

It is good fun all the same and as much instructive to me as it is to them for, they receive all their lessons in Urdu and amazingly enough, I can follow every word.

In a few weeks they will have advanced so far that they will be able to read and write, drill in a way that wouldn't disgrace the guards and then they will learn to drive, and other recruits will cast envious eyes in their direction.

New Recruits

Promotion to Lieutenant
– still 28-2.43

From tomorrow I'm a <u>Lt</u> but as it has not yet appeared in orders, I cannot put up the second pip or use the title.

Little matter-, the pay (another £3–£4 a month) dates from March 1ˢᵗ and I'm told that is the most important thing. George and I celebrated the occasion (for him too) by going out to the flicks last night and followed it up with a dinner.

And then just two weeks later the big posting – orders to join 589 TANK TRANSPORTER COMPANY. A British Company assigned to the 14ᵗʰ ARMY.

MARCH '43

Address – 589 Tank Transporter Co, RASC, India Command
14-3-43
This is my first Sunday in my new home. My surroundings are just about as different to any previous ones as they could be – being much more like those in Egypt where there were miles and miles of sweet nothing, cloudless skies and blazing sun.

That is roughly what it is like except that the sand is displaced with a kind of gravel and there are actually trees dotted about every quarter mile or so on average.

Living conditions are quite good though. I share a room of a hut with a chap I knew in Kakul, electric light thrown in – who can complain? A big point is remembering the six blankets I was using a couple of months ago – now a mosquito net and one sheet are ample, too much in fact!

A permanent posting
You can regard this address as permanent.

I'm fixed up for good and have a job which is going to keep me really busy – every Indian in the Company is mine and mine alone and as they seem to include every type and creed in existence the fun and games are only just beginning. **What we are, who we are, where we are and why we are, are all taboo – so look forward to some highly enlightening letters describing the weather!**[10]

The middle of nowhere!
The following is taken from the extended letter 'I was there and how!'
written in April 1945:
Dhond if not the last place on earth is at least the next station up the line. My railway ticket said it was 965 miles from Delhi and I'm surprised it's as near as that.

You've had some varied train journeys; I've described some; but to do justice to the flies, the heat, dust and colour of that southbound trip, calls for a better manipulator of Encyclopaedia Britannica than I – words fail me.

Boy, but it was hot, even though it was March. India floated passed the carriage, the usual galaxy of mountains, big rivers, water buffalo, temples,

---

10 What we find out later, in a letter written in 1945, is that he was in a place called Dhond, that the chap he knew in Kakul was in fact to be his senior officer and was a huge help in his new role - transporting tanks, munitions, troops and supplies across India in preparation for things to come.

chattering monkeys, beggars, forests, deserts, char and egg wallas, fakirs, family men and foaming colonels.

At last, it made up its mind; a barren, desolate waste, miles of sandy coloured nothing, scattered clumps of cactus and scrub dotted places where the dry earth had settled in the crevices of the rocks; a tree was an object of interest; mirages of water were common; sand spouts wavered gracefully across the vista.

In the middle of this I found Dhond – simply there because a river has misguidedly meandered through the waste, making a patch of green which stretched at least one hundred yards from the railway station; my company was three miles away. Poona 50.

The New Unit

As you can imagine, the feeling on joining any new unit is one of strangeness – what are the officers going to be like, and the men. I assure you to join a **British Unit** for the first time, even if half the strength is Indian, to know that the Sergeant Major has probably had more leave than you have had service, knowing how little you know, gives a feeling of the squeemies second to none. I should know!

But then I met Syd. Oh yes, introductions, meet Syd, a little man with a big laugh. Syd meet Mamselle X, the Great Unknown. There, now you can come aboard. Sydney Hawes, half pint size, ex sergeant major with, when necessary, a voice to match. 28, prematurely bald, shiny eyes and a big grin who had been at Kakul with us and had left Delhi a few days ahead of me to become 2 i/c of this new company. I was at home at once.

It was at this stage in my travels that I became mobile – no more bicycles or tongas, I had a 15cwt truck of my own and roads, not railways became the connection between A and B.

My mileage, which, since then has rarely dropped below 1000 per month, began immediately – I had to teach about 80 junglies to drive, to learn to drive a thirty-ton transporter myself and then again, pass that knowledge to the thugs.

Time flew by and apart from a weekly route march the bareness of the surrounding country didn't worry us unduly: however, each evening after the days blazing heat a strong wind would blow across the flat waste – a wind almost solid, that penetrated everywhere – not so good.

APRIL '43

4-4-43

I'm settled in now and am beginning to know my men by name, a thing which I always insist I must know but which presents a 'biggish' task.

April 1ˢᵗ (Fools Day) was a super one for me as it was the first, I've had off since my arrival – Sundays are working days for me these days – I'm now Mess President in addition to other duties and I went to the nearest town on a combined business and shopping expedition.

I came back loaded with footballs, volleyballs, hockey balls, glasses and tumblers, books, writing materials, drink and many other things and I think I can say we have a completely contented company at present.

Things Going Well
18-4-43

Well, everything is still as good as ever. I'm fit and busy, the news is cheering and I've some new pals to fill in the leisure moments, two from London which is quite a change as previously my pals always seemed to be from the Midlands or the North.

My junglies are doing well too and are good lads to command: together we have built about 5 miles of road in the last few days for a driving course and now they tootle round in fine fettle. The fact that I end up each day covered from head to foot in mud and dust, it having been blown in clouds all over the course, doesn't worry us much A bath in a tin tub and a change of clothing soon puts things right.

589 Company. March 1943

MAY '43

Things continue into May – a trip to Poona being the only unusual event. Then, on the way back:

The First sign of 'The Monsoon'

It had been oppressive all day and after covering ten miles of bumpy road back, the heavens simply burst – the monsoon had arrived in strength.

All the land in view, visibility was reduced to about a hundred yards, seemed to be flowing away; slopes were alive, ditches gushing; a culvert under the road, unable to cope, sending a stream of water over the tarmac.

As we crossed a bridge, a rickety wooden structure running parallel to it, was washed away: the road, where it crossed the river bed on an Irish bridge [*i.e. a bridge for low water flow only*], was two feet under water and the truck was swept sideways until it struck the concrete pillars put there for just such an emergency.

We were stuck. Half an hour later the storm ceased, as if a tap had been turned off – the flow of water decreased almost at once and we were able to continue.

Before we reached our camp, the only relic of the storm was a fresh, earthy smell, pervading the atmosphere – there wasn't a drop of water to be seen.

THE GREAT TREK

Two days later we left on the 'great trek': across India by road, with the monsoon chasing us all the way.[11]

Each evening, before we left and for the first three days of the convoy we had violent rain and thunderstorms as the clouds brewed up after the mid-days' heat.

After the third day, we out-distanced the weather and ran into heat and oppressiveness which always precedes the rains – thermometers wobbling between 110 -120 degrees in the shade!

Just as they are now!!

The Route

Got a map pal? You might like to trace our wanderings across the face of the world. **Dhond, Poona, Ahmednager, Mhow, Jhansi** (yes again!) **Cawnpore, Allabad, Benares, down the Delhi – Calcutta trunk road, Hajaribagh, to Ranch**i.

1400 odd miles for the convoy, 2075 for Towny in 22 days.

My Role

I had all the fun: my truck was loaded to capacity, seven of us with our kit and I had to travel ahead to make all the necessary arrangements for those behind.

Parking area for two hundred vehicles, food, petrol, water (not easy to find sometimes), ice to prevent heat stroke, rivers to wash in, entertainment and to find the way out of the larger cities!

It was super! We saw India as it should be seen, from the dusty roads, with us, at times, living on the land – chickens, eggs, milk and fruit purchased on the way. I saw every town we passed through thoroughly, riding up and down the streets till we had seen them all; we stopped in the middle of no-where when distances became impossible.

A dispatch rider who broke his leg gave us the opportunity to run into **Mhow** the night before the convoy arrived – a chance which we took, to live in the Dak bungalow like lords, iced beer, lovely grub, everything.

---

11 Copies of some of the 'secret orders' that covered 'The Great Trek' are included in the Appendix

Incidentally the Dak bungalow is an Indian institution – there is one in every town; a place where anybody can get a nights lodging and, if it is a large one, food. As there are few, or no hotels on the roads (rail is the normal means of covering such distance) these bungalows fill an essential gap.

Anyway, we rose late in the morning and still had time to make all arrangements and see the town too. The convoy arrived and settled in about midday and Towny discreetly faded away to the bazaar on a shopping expedition and thence to the flicks!

The convoy was staying in town the next day for maintenance on the vehicles and the lads were roped in for early morning PT – I was quarter-bloke, slid out on an early trip to the supply depot and military dairy farm to collect fresh butter and fresh meat – a welcome change after the tinned varieties – and was so pleased with myself that I almost ran down the dairy farm's prize mad bull!

Suddenly sobered up I went hastily into reverse and sat in the cab until the 'old-fashioned' stares were over and the bull rumbled off – coo, I thought I'd bought it – and at 7 am too!

Local Discussions!

Later in the day we departed for the next stage, a village miles from anywhere in which the military had never been and if they were wise, would never stop again.

Next morning, I indicated that I would have speech with the local potentate and was duly escorted by two thugs in scarlet uniforms and dangling swords into a room which was only remarkable for the frowstiness of the pictures on the wall and the ordinariness of the half dozen occupants – all male – no faithful slaves, dancing girls or nowt.

I, somewhat deflated, was giving my Urdu a mental polish when the smallest and most insignificant guy squawked in the most perfect English:

"Where do you propose to put your convoy?"

That was definitely below the belt – point No 1 – he shouldn't have been able to speak English and point No 2 – I'd come to see him about drinking water and where I was parking the wagons was my business – so I thought.

Apparently, it wasn't, and they were most interested, and it took me half an hour to convince them that I'd chosen the only possible place – but if they cared to give me two hundred coolies I'd try to make it probable that half a dozen trucks could use their site. Round No 1 to me!

About the water, it wasn't so good – they went into a wordy clinch between themselves, making much of the fact that the monsoon was late, and the country was suffering from drought; 'Bannerjees Well' was almost dry and 'Chatterjees Well' was supplying the village – we could use a third, but they weren't sure if the water was drinkable.

My! My! The tact it took for me to tell Indians about their own weather – that the monsoon wasn't late but early, only two days ago I'd seen it down the road!

And the greater point that they could not risk poisoning the first British troops to stay on their domain – it wouldn't look 'quaite naice'!

I felt weak when I staggered out: weaker still when I found that the convoy had arrived, and the lads were rapidly emptying the only good well in the village! I pulled out at once before the local constabulary started checking fingerprints!

Jhansi, of course, I knew – and also by shooting a line to the new OC Supply Depot – telling him how things were done in the good old days (he said, 'Oh yes, Townsend, I remember that some of the vouchers you signed were returned for correction!')

I extracted an issue of mineral water for the lads. I can tell you pardner, my stock was pretty good for the next few days – in fact until I couldn't get any bread and we had to resort to biscuits – but could I get those empty bottles back?

If I was the kinda fella who let things get him down, I'd still have sleepless nights on account of them doggorned bottles – in fact I'm still awaiting the bill charging me lakhs [*1 lakh = 100,000*] of rupees for those I couldn't find after laying booby traps and raiding vehicle toolboxes.

'The Mobile Madhouse'

It was at about this stage that iced melon was introduced into the 'Horaces Hotstuff' Travelling Hotel or as some unenlightened being so crushingly put it 'The Mobile Madhouse'.

There were plenty of melons available in the villages – big football watermelons, lashings of blood red flesh and black pips and 'my type' – cantaloupes, luscious, orange 'meat', simply gushing juice, right and left. There was also 'the anti – heatstroke' ice – the combination was perfect – stop slavering at the jaws, Lizzie!

And so, it came to pass that on one fair day, we, having decided on the pitch, dallied by the wayside to dangle our feet in a nearby river and to lazily munch our way through a pile of melons.

It was a dreamy sort of day, life seemed so good, the water was soothing to my Sergeant's corn. (I can still picture the look of dumb rapture smarmed across his pan), the birds were twittering, and twits were nattering when one of the intelligentsia who had his eyes open (must have had tummy trouble after too much melon) said:

"Cor lumme, there aren't arf a lot of wagons going up the road."

We all peeked an eye in the direction suggested, closed them again, murmured "yes you're quite right there are a lot" and settled down to dream of re-patriation as usual.

Then suddenly, the truth, as only the truth can, DAWNED. Towny had one of those moments, all too rare, thank the Lord, when he was inspired – he actually thought and was almost knocked flat by the effort. With glazy eyes and choking voice he announced for the benefit of the Seven Sinners – wrong, Six Sleepers- **'They're ours – get cracking!'**

We cracked.

Boots were wrenched on, though I later found that my driver didn't worry to fix his and drove the next few miles barefooted; trousers hitched and scattered, kit collected, and we were away – to reach the main road and see as far as we could see, in both directions, vehicles by the dozen, battling along at a speed, far in excess of the convoy 'twenty per', and with, so it seemed, an appointment to keep in Tokyo.

We cracked – flat out and passed them one by one and eventually overtook the leader, leaving him in such a cloud of dust that he didn't know it was us anyway.

At the first possible place up the road, we nipped out, put out our guides and nonchalantly waved the wagons into their new parking place – just two minutes old/Phew!

Lucky for us that nine tenths of India is so barren and useless! Luck was with me too as we found a well not far from the site and I was able to overcome the OC's tart remarks on map reading by reminding him that I was using an 'All India' road map at 50 miles to the inch and if he would persist on using it to swat flies, who was I to tell the difference between flies' blood and roads! I quell 'em! But my, my, it was a near thing that, Henrietta.

Local customs

So, we went on.: **Cawnpore** [*now Kanpur, Upper Pradesh*] a nice city, poor flicks, good beer, and hard to find the way out of: **Allahabad,** spent another maintenance day there, at the confluence of the Ganges and then **Jumma,** two mighty rivers combining to make a miniature ocean.

More local griff: – if a Hindu washes his body in the combined waters, all the past dirty deeds are nix [*nothing/no more*] – he comes up with a sheet cleaner than any sent to Belinda's Bob Bagwash and can start his fun and games all over again. My, but there's a lot of people wash themselves!

Better still, if a guy should die on the banks just here and again at **Benares**, a hundred odd miles down the line, his soul goes right up to the higher levels by the cheap midday excursion, no stops no restaurant car, no nothing.

It'd make you grin to see the thousands of lads in their mis-spent second youths, backing the tote both ways – living on the riverbank until they die and taking a daily bath to keep the linen clean. I should know – I nearly joined 'em!

Making History!

For someone like yourself the colossal road- rail bridges over the Ganges at both Benares and Allahabad would be of interest.

Me, I like quantity as well as quality and found it at a place not marked on any normal map – **Dehri-on-Sone** [*on the Sone River, a tributary of the Ganges*].

The village doesn't deserve such a high-sounding name, but I wandered up to the local station master (an Anglo-Indian from Liverpool Cantonment [*i.e. garrison*] whom I'd been told to contact and asked for the dope on his bridge (he emphasised the 'his' repeatedly).

When asked if he had a bridge he neatly remarked "Oh, I 'ave 'em all, that's it over there, lad" – and I looked down the railway line until I hit the horizon but could see no bridge – it looked quite an ordinary bit of line to me.

So, I walked a hundred yards in direction A to point B – and thought I'd reached the Sahara. The land dropped about thirty feet to the riverbed; the bridge went on and on and on for two and a half miles!

Hoping to renew the polish on the line I'd shot about the Middle East, I suggested to my Sergeant (that long suffering man) that we should go and find the **River Sone** – it must be somewhere in the middle of its sand. It was – a mile from the bank, a mere hundred yards of it and what looked like another mile of sand on the other side. We were not impressed!

And that evening, never-to-be-repeated history was made, we took our convoy across the bridge, wearing away tyres, rubbing against the rails, wearing away the drivers' tempers, by such continued high concentration upon their job – but later came a complaint from the railway people that we were wearing away their 'railway lines', or at least displacing them so, thereafter no wagons were driven across and all had to be loaded on to the railway trucks for a three-mile journey! **History has been made!**

We reached nowhere the next evening – we simply stopped by the roadside thirty miles from the nearest large village and settled down for the night.

On arrival there hadn't been a person or a house in sight, just a well and a clump of trees. Half an hour later, to an audience of about two hundred, I demonstrated how an English Rajah Sahib uses a razor to remove the jolly old face fungus.

Where everyone had come from is still a mystery to me, but they gazed at us as if we'd just arrived from Mars – on second thoughts maybe they were Martians – blood-thirsty blighters too! You should have heard them cheer when I drew blood. (My own, damn it!).

Iced dust remover!

It was at this juncture that I was rudely interrupted in my cursing by the OC, who suggested I should 'slip' into the next town to get the daily 'ice' in case anyone should go down with 'the heat' (I thought it a good idea as I'd had the odd iced noggin with him the previous evening).

I slipped – 75 miles there and back – arriving in camp at 10.30 pm and most of the ice melted!

Everyone had turned in, so I and my motley crew revived ourselves with a nice, iced dust remover apiece, tucked into the new days melon ration and took a very good view of things all around.

We'd seen another town, off the route, kept cool by jangling steadily along through the hot 'airless' evening and we'd had our nightcap just as the doctor ordered.

We left camp before the others roused themselves in the morning as we wished to see the next halting place – **Benares**, as well as avoid an 'ice –less' rumpus!

Holy customs

Actually, I saw very little of the Hindus Holy City; it took me a long time to find a way into it and then to return and lead the convoy in – then again to find a way out, show it to guides; collect food, petrol and other necessaries and to visit a pal who worked in the supply depot.

The lads who went sight-seeing confirmed all previous reports of the place: hosts of people bathing away their sins in the Ganges, burning ghats [*steps leading down to the river*], where bodies of those lucky enough to peg out on the river-side are cremated, temples, temple dancers, fakirs, sadhus (holy men who make a good living out of a piece of sacking, a head covered with ashes and a begging bowl – no one likes to pass them without putting something in the porridge basin – and crowds who were there simply because 'there's no charge for looking.'

Besides, some of these Indian religious sects have some funny customs, which are interesting. One mob, known as the **Jains**, believe, amongst other things, that no living thing should be killed – just left to die naturally. So, these odd people won't put their foot on spare beetles, or swat flies, kill animals for food or anything normal.

The Parsees are fire worshippers and another gang have a couple of bright ways of making sure that their souls reach the higher levels intact.

Method number one is to chuck the corpse into the Ganges – it's a holy river to begin with, which helps a lot in these manners – the theory is that the fish eat the body, birds eat the fish and fly, with the inner spirit, heavenwards, and Bob's your Uncle.

No 2 cuts out the first stage – the body is put on an iron grill; the vultures do the rest, and the bones fall through into the pit below. But I'm warning you I've not seen it underway – and I've no wish to either.

WVS to the Rescue!

There was only one other outstanding incident on the trip – I reached a lovely spot called **Hazaribagh** (trans: a thousand gardens – and it was!), fixed up everything nicely and settled down for the convoy to come: It didn't!

Rather annoyed I went back thirty miles to look for it and found that one of the lads had carelessly broken a bridge and the rest were fording a river – very, very slowly and would not finish in one day. Too bad, as I'd fixed up with a canteen to lay on a 'do' for us – quite a change as the English of India rarely put themselves out for passing troops.

Inspiration came! If the boys can't come to the canteen, we'll bring the canteen to them.

I whistled back with a couple of trucks, suggested to the local WVS [*Women's Voluntary Service*] that a trip in the country would do them a lot of good (and us!) and the idea went down well.

Half the residents of the town turned out (about 30!!) and we made it an all-night party, leaving their canteen stocks in much the same condition as a plague of locusts would. My stock was up again – above par, and we had a few contacts which proved useful later, when we passed through on other convoys.

JUNE '43

Ranchi

And so, we came to **Ranchi**, my home for the next 4 1/2 months. I was no
very impressed as we rolled into our new camp. It was greener than a lot we
had seen but was nothing outstanding.

We pitched our tents, moved some lads into the newly created bamboo and
grass huts and settled down for the first full night's sleep for almost a month

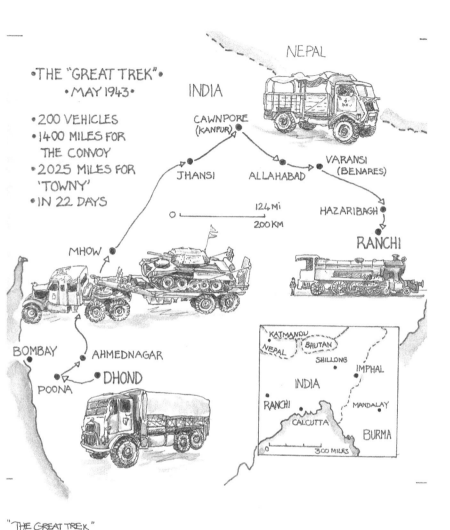

The following text labels appear within the illustration:

- THE "GREAT TREK"
- MAY 1943
- 200 VEHICLES
- 1400 MILES FOR THE CONVOY
- 2025 MILES FOR 'TOWNY'
- IN 22 DAYS

NEPAL
INDIA
CAWNPORE (KANPUR)
JHANSI
ALLAHABAD
VARANSI (BENARES)
HAZARIBAGH
RANCHI
MHOW
124 Mi
200 KM
BOMBAY
AHMEDNAGAR
POONA
DHOND

Inset map:
KATMANDU
NEPAL
BHUTAN
SHILLONG
IMPHAL
INDIA
RANCHI
MANDALAY
CALCUTTA
BURMA
300 MILES

"THE GREAT TREK"
21·2·21   SAL TOWNSEND ©

The Great Trek

CHAPTER 10

Tanks, Trains and Transfer – to Imphal

July – December 1943

JULY '43

A very wet welcome

The monsoon arrived in Ranchi shortly after we did, just like that! It had caught up on us and as usual, the rain was torrential. Three of the huts collapsed, tents were blown over, water was everywhere – need I say more.

The next week was spent in digging ditches in between storms – but on the other-hand the countryside was wonderful to behold.

After the first rain, the rice in the paddy fields shot up – turning the brown fields into a sheet of emerald green: the rain made a useful lake too and when our homes had finally been made waterproof, we began to take a good view of things.

Ranchi possesses a bazaar of the higher quality, two cinemas with hard seats but fairly up-to-date films, a club with a billiard table and good roads – we were happy.

Monthly Mileage Up and Up

Monthly mileage went up and up – our clients [*i.e., tanks, tank crews etc*] were training and we had to make long convoys regularly – on top of which we had to collect new vehicles and train my Indians. Lots of times we bogged vehicles – they look like battleships sinking and had some rare fun in extracting them out of the mud.

Once I ran a convoy down a road as far as a bridge which said, '9 tons max!' – we weighed 30 tons! I suppose you've seen a transporter – maybe you can imagine the problem turning them round in a twenty-foot road – we had to turn 15 of the blighters with rain pelting down and most unpleasant.

Leave, tanks and trains

Those that could went on leave. Robbie, another of my brethren, went to hospital, Syd went to visit him. Robbie is getting married this year to the sister who nursed him, Syd nearly married three different girls, then happened to remember he has a wife back home – we had a very pleasant time!

Actually, life was so full of variety I can't recall any major items. 589 farms were started – monkeys, goats, dogs, pigeons and for a short while, a young deer. Motor-bike picnics at several of the local waterfalls; unloading trains; working all night.

I've got it! It was at this stage in my misspent youth that I was able to satisfy the wildest dream of every twentieth century kid – I drove a railway train. Moreover, I shunted wagons up and down sidings by day and night.

In fact, I was just about to apply for my 'A' licence when I climbed aboard a big passenger engine – it didn't look so easy after all, my tanker being a modified Rocket!

Between you and me and anyone else whose listening, train driving isn't all it's cracked up to be – I mean to say, 'What's your idea of Hell?' Stoking up great fires? Which would seem to make a train driver's job a mere hell on earth – my idea exactly.

It's hot, it's dirty, there are no padded seats to sit on – it's uncomfortable, the hours are long and the track becomes very monotonous – and most engine drivers have to work their way through the ranks of cleaner's mate, stoker uppers and so on – hotter, dirtier jobs. No, I'm sticking to roads and cars – they are at least <u>cold</u> and only dirty sometimes!

Which again reminds me (for heaven's sake stop the man someone!) I drove tanks for the first time during this working vacation – big ones and little ones – to the horror of everyone present.

I'm sorry to say I ran over the local villagers' burial spot – there was no indication to say 'Here lies poor old Abdul Khan and his Misses Eliza', no fences, flowers, tombstones or anything – just countryside.

I jangled around in fantastic patterns, climbed out of the turret to accept the congratulations on my performance, in my most modest and nonchalant manner

– then hurled myself to one side as the owner of the tank endeavoured to revenge himself and turned round to meet -- farsends and farsends of violent villagers!

Ooh they <u>were</u> annoyed, and it took at least half an hour working back along the pedigree of each family and pointing out the space allotted to great, great granfer Akbar and each of his progeny.

It faded out with profuse apologies, but it seemed that the damage was already done – the next day they opened up a spot of ground I'd already loosened for them and popped in a nicely wrapped-up corpse – they assured me it was the first burial in the village for five years – and ever since I've had a vague feeling that I must have hastened the old boy on his way with shock!

And on to convoy after convoy

Everyone who was anyone thought it was high time that Towny was gainfully occupied, as my esteemed buddy Bill Beveridge so aptly put it, so off I went on convoy after convoy. It was smashing, the monsoon had ended, it was cool and clear, the countryside perfect.

It had to end though – the company had to move on, and the OC said, 'DT old chap, you had a pretty good trip last time – this time you can take all the spare bodies by rail."

What a memory that man possessed! So, the wagons rolled away, leaving Syd, Robbie and myself to create a lasting impression on the residents of Ranchi and I feel sure the folks must have considered our departure as good as a course of monkey gland treatment – we put years on 'em!

DECEMBER 1943

I left a week after the trucks, with three English lads and about a hundred Indians, for a place that I'd never heard of before – Imphal.

It was only just on my map of India and it was rumoured that from this outpost of the Empire, violent war was being waged against the Japs – and it was up to us to find out.

Thirty miles to the railway station, only to find that our train was due to leave the following day, didn't seem a very successful commencement. Nor, having slept in the open, did the fact that the dew had soaked us during the night, create a feeling of wellbeing. Anyway, things brightened up when we'd fed, bundled all the junglies into the carriages and started on our way.

Brighter still were we, when, after a fairly speedy mornings run, we saw a number of our vehicles halted by the wayside – they had been stuck there for a week! It later came out that because a bridge had been washed away by the monsoon floods, our vehicles had to go by rail – but there weren't enough trucks! Some arrived 6 weeks later!!

My BORs [*British Other Officers*] and I travelled most of the way on the engine – we even stoked a bit and made toast on a shovel full of embers extracted from the firebox – and it helped relieve the monotony of the journey. I think it took us 3 or 4 days to cover the three hundred miles to the **Brahmaputra** – halting in sidings for hours on end – to arrive in a rest camp in the dark [*the Brahmaputra river- a trans-boundary river which flows through Tibet, India and Bangladesh. Its big - the 9th largest river in the world by discharge. They would have been at the crossing within India*].

The next stage of the trip was tops – three days in a river steamer going up the river – fogbound each morning, cool breezes during the day and wonderful sunsets over the water at night. We had nothing to do except sit and watch the water slipping passed and cook high meals a-la Mrs Beaton – what a life!

Two more days to reach the railhead were not quite as pleasant as the rolling stock was antiquated and each rail seemed to be half an inch lower than the previous one (that or the wheels weren't round!).

Then came the ride of my life! The first viewing of the **Manipur Road** - from the back of a three tonner!

Have I ever described the road to you, pardner? Starting at 1000' – climbing to six and ending at two thousand – in a hundred miles there isn't a hundred yards that is straight – big drops one side, high cliffs the other – cloud covered in the high spots, hot and sticky lower down – at the time the surface was rotten – so were the drivers.

In the back of a lorry one feels every bump in the road, the swaying is accentuated, the petrol fumes create a choking sensation. I've a strong stomach – some of my lads hadn't!!

Arrival at Imphal

Again we arrived in the dark – the OC, as I awoke him, greeted me with 'Oh – its you' then as the cogs creaked, 'Good Lord – where have you come from?' – as if he didn't know.

I had it seemed, passed most of the wagons and the old man had only been in the area a couple of days himself – and it kinda looked as if I'd dropped in when he had only one bottle left, hence the welcome.

He fixed me! The next morning he took me round a piece of bamboo covered country and said, "Our camp will be here – we'll live in those bashes – allot it out to platoons and properly organise everything – I'll live in there."

I walked 'in there' just to see what he'd picked for himself, giving a polite "Salaam" to the Manipuri squatting on the doorstep - and, in the almost pitch dark of the interior, nearly fell on top of a woman feeding a baby, a pile of other sqatting brats and a couple of chickens.

Retracing my steps, thoughtful like, I asked him if he knew the huts were occupied.

"Oh yes – I forgot to tell you – you've got to clear the village first" – just like that!

So I again did an about turn and to the crowd who'd assembled matily enquired "Does anyone speak English?"

The silence was very, very deep – too deep in fact. I repeated the question in Urdu – the silence became deeper – really you could have sunk the Queen Mary in it and still have had a lot of depth left – I'd had it!

So I sat down on the next doorstep and to no-one in particular said in Urdu, "It's a nice day. How are you?" Imagine my surprise when the other doorstep squatter agreed, in the most pedantic English!

"Yes, it is a fine day. I am quite well. How are you please?"

Tell me – what does one do in such circumstances – I have a feeling I made goldfish noises as I tried to get enough breath for normal conversation. He beat me to it.

"It would suit you Sir if we left tomorrow? The Maharajah said the military would come and we would have to move."

I recovered – assured him that tomorrow would do fine and I'd let him have some men to help him – and the camp was built. Then it was Christmas – and the start of my Imphal experience was underway!

PART 3

The Battle of Imphal

December 1943 – July 1944

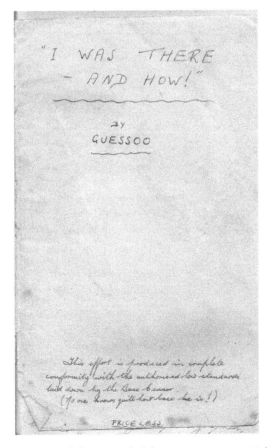

The cover of the extended letter written in 1945
The title – 'I was there and how' says it all!

CHAPTER 11

Background and Battle Plans

Background

Before getting back to 'The Letters' let me make you aware of what was happening in the war in and around Imphal at the time that Dad arrived in December 1943. First an explanation of the respective plans of the Japanese and the Allies, coupled with an explanation of why Imphal was the place where all this was happening.

THE JAPANESE PLANS

Imphal is the capital of Manipur, one of five states in the extreme North East of India. It is on a high plain directly to the north of Myanmar (Burma) and has high mountains to east and west. The natural route through these mountains leads from Imphal to Kohima and then to the rich farming lands of Assam. Some have termed Imphal 'The Front Door to India'.

The Tokyo Government had told their commander in Burma, General Masakazu Kawabe, that there must be 'no bad news from him in 1944'. Burma was, by now, very much under Japanese control and Kawabe's aim was to capitalise on this and make the move on India. There was sufficient unrest in India to provide support if he could just get through to its main cities. His plan, his best chance of success, was to advance from the Chindwin, to capture the Imphal plateau and Kohima and to continue his thrust north from there.

He realised that the mountains provided a natural defence from approaches from India proper; he believed that the large rice crop of Assam would be available for his army and that his troops could live and supply themselves from the Allies' dumps and bases. He also planned to upset counter-offensive preparations by launching raids and use guerrillas and spies of the 'Indian Traitor Army' (formed from prisoners taken in Malaya) to send word to Assam and Eastern Bengal, where revolutionary cadres stood ready to co-operate with them.

The timescale allotted to this by Kawabe was just three weeks!

A second major element of Kawabe's plan was to deceive the Allies, to make them believe that Imphal was NOT his main objective. He arranged to launch an attack in the south, through the eastern coastlands of Arakan, heading to India via Chittagong and Calcutta. It would be a large enough assault to appear to be the main Japanese offensive and to draw troops away from his main objective - the Imphal plateau. Kawabe would start this in February '44 with the Imphal offensive starting, 300 miles away, one month later.

THE ALLIES PLANS

Whilst the battle of Imphal did not start until March '44, Dad's arrival in December '43 along with many other troops was very much a part of the forward preparation by the Allies. It also coincided with a number of recent changes in the Allies organisation and command:

SEAC – Lord Mountbatten

South East Asia Command (SEAC) had been formed in November '43 under the command of Admiral Lord Louis Mountbatten. SEAC took over control and operations from India Command. Mountbatten proved to be an inspirational leader and gave a new vitality and urgency to all aspects of the retake of Burma and defeat of the Japanese.

Dad's address from arriving in Imphal changed from 'India Command' to 'South East Asia Command'.

Lt General William Slim

Slim had been involved in the retreat in 1942 and was appointed commander of the newly formed 14th Army in the Autumn of 1943. Slim was an excellent leader, well respected by soldiers at every level and he firmly believed that Burma could be retaken by overland forces. This was very much against the conventional military wisdom of the time and it was his vision and belief that the strength of the Allied forces, particularly their superiority in combined arms and tanks warfare, could be decisive.

His vision was not without a true sense of reality too. It was clear that there was a massive task ahead. Malaria, dysentery, jungle warfare and communications had all proved to be as significant adversaries as the Japanese themselves. Emphasis was placed on all aspects of training for Jungle warfare and on developing more aggressive tactics using increased air support. His excellent leadership skills and energetic approach was fully committed from the start into building the 14ᵗʰ Army into a fighting force capable of achieving victory.

Lt D.A.Townsend

Perhaps not quite as important as those responsible for the overall strategy and tactics employed but, in his role as a Lieutenant in a specialist transport company, he was certainly a lot more involved in 'making it happen' than I had ever imagined.

All his training to date, in supplies and as a specialist in tank transport and convoys, had been geared to him becoming a much needed asset in the difficult times ahead. Interestingly, due to the specialist nature of the training and the length of time that it took, further promotion was not allowed for such Lieutenants until peace was finally declared in August 1945.

As he arrives in Imphal he talks of 'taking certain things to certain places' which de-coded means tanks, ammunition, supplies and troops to the front line. Four months later 'we had the honour of collecting up some of theirs' – (meaning he was collecting Japanese tanks from the battlefields) and with his special touch of humour makes light of it, describing how he made a Japanese flag out of his pyjamas and flew it at the head of the convoy so that 'our chaps didn't think the battered tin cans were ours!'. He had plenty of big money offers for that flag!

The Transport Company was a key part of the 14ᵗʰ Army. Whilst Dad was delivering tanks to the battlefields from the Imphal end of 'our road', his friend Robbie and other members of the same company were doing the same job based in Kohima. Their celebrations when they eventually met were worthy of the occasion.

Not to take any enjoyment away from the story ahead, but as a quick insight of what is to come, I can tell you that on one occasion his jeep was overturned by an exploding bomb and another bomb caused him to jump naked from his (tin) bath into his own 'box' (a 7' x 5' x 3.5' pit) for protection.

I tell you all this now because, reading the letters, you might not appreciate just how dangerous his situation was and just what a terrible battle it was to be. The fighting went on for four months and many now hold it to be a greater turning point in WW2 than any other battle. Tens of thousands were killed or wounded.

In the letters it is rare for any sense of danger, fear, or complaint to feature. The sense of adventure and humour is far more to the fore – but I think it is important to understand the setting in which the letters were written to really appreciate what Dad and so many others accomplished in the most difficult of circumstances.

Wingate and the Chindits

It was not until the world heard about Wingate and the Chindits (British and Gurkha forces using 'guerrilla warfare' tactics to go deep behind enemy lines) in early 1943, that the ongoing war in Burma received some of the publicity that it deserved. Only later did the whispered stories of heavy casualties start to circulate.

Wingate was a non-conformist commander who had success with Long Range penetration techniques in the Abyssinian campaign, serving under General Wavell. Wavell had been in command in Burma in the earlier part of 1943 and agreed to use the same techniques here. Losses were heavy but both Churchill and Roosevelt endorsed a large expansion of these techniques in 1944. This was to be coupled with greater use of air support for all ground troops.

In the event, Wingate was killed in an airplane accident when taking off from Imphal in March '44. Command of the Chindits was given to one General Lentaigne who used the forces to back up the Americans and Chinese rather than their original long-range purpose.

As a result more traditional tactics, including tank warfare in which Dad was so involved, became even more important than had been expected.

To Complete the Picture

Allied intelligence got word of the Japanese plans to invade Imphal and of their deceptive plans in Arakan. Field Marshall Slim appreciated that the Centre was the vital sector and, with the blessing of Mountbatten, withdrew 4 Corps from its forward position to the Imphal plain and there he prepared to receive a Japanese attack.

This shortened the Allies lines of communication while lengthening those of the Japanese. It meant that Slim's main bases, supply and ammunition depots and supporting airfields lay very close to his back whilst the Japanese would have a supply line of over 200 miles.

Again with Mountbatten's blessing, Slim had arranged for massive air support for his troops, both in Arakan and at Imphal. A final change was that when communications or supplies were cut off, his troops were not to retreat as they had done before; they were to dig in and await air supplies.

This worked. Arakan (300 miles away from Imphal) was a tough but successful victory for the Allies. An extract from 'Orders of the Day' issued on 29th February 1944 from Lord Louis reads:

'You have given the Japanese a crack they will remember. Three weeks ago, the enemy sent a large and formidable force through the jungle to cut your lines

of communication and attack you in the rear. You have met the onslaught with courage, confidence and resolution. The enemy forces which infiltrated have been destroyed and scattered. The threatened passes are clear, the roads are open. You have gained complete victory'.

And so, to Imphal

To quote again from E.D Smith's 'Battle for Burma': 'the grim struggle in Arakan, the imaginative penetrations by Special Forces, all of these were preliminary but important sideshows to the death struggle that was to be waged with relentless fury around Imphal between **March – July 1944**. *It was to be the most decisive battle of the campaign in South East Asia'*

And now back to 'The Letters'.

CHAPTER 12

'I was There and How'

December '43 – May '44

The heading 'I was there and how' is taken from the 34-page booklet that Dad wrote whilst in a field hospital in April '45. It seemed fitting to use it here given just how much he was going to be involved in the coming battle.

IMPHAL – DECEMBER '43

Settling In

Of course, you will be itching to know where, why and how I am. The last is easy I'm really fine, I've never been quite so healthy, hungry, tired or busy – 'flat out' is the only term which conveys the idea of how life is at present.

'Where' and 'why', will remain a 'great unknown' until the days of our fireside chats –got to keep the censor happy! One thing – I can speak to the locals better than Jai Lal [*his Indian batman*] – as they don't understand much Urdu and I can now count up to ten in English, Welsh, German, French, Esperanto, Arabic and Urdu – how's that!

The weather is now lovely during the day and although it keeps clear and starry at night it is bitterly cold. I sleep on my camp bed with a valise and six thicknesses of blanket below me and 3 blankets and a greatcoat and valise flaps on top – like a bug in a rug – and I don't like leaving it to shave in icy water in the mornings.

I live next to a lot of cows (real ones) who are rather noisy sleepers. I've fixed myself with an electric light from a car battery and inspection lamp suitably blacked out – and I use it on occasions such as this when I write letters on my table (an empty tea chest!). There, you have my home in one and it's one I'm glad to creep back to after a day's work.

I've now really palled up with a family of the 'locals' – they have built me a huge 'charpoy' (bed) of bamboo which I am going to test tonight. It looks a beauty, but I know I'll go to sleep so quickly and deeply that it won't be appreciated for some time.

These locals are very friendly in spite of language difficulties and they sit on my doorstep (there's no door) and watch me shave, dress and everything else. At odd times they present me with a length of sugar cane or a bowl of icy cold (crushed) sugar juice – very tasty!'

Oh, so busy!
9-12-43
Please excuse the delay (I warned you of it) and the haste in which this is written but here are just a few lines from the wide-open spaces to let you know I'm quite ok and exceedingly busy.

The lack of mail is bound to continue as we are not yet halfway 'backwards or forwards' but I'll write just as often as I can fit in.

At present I'm once again engaged in making history and you'll have to wait until times are normal again – still, I'm enjoying the experience greatly and as I said am kept on the go all the time.

About a week ago I saw a place that reminded me greatly of Faygate[12] – now, even that is a few hundred miles behind and we are looking forward to an Xmas dinner of bamboo shoots!

I've spent a lot of time on footplates of railway locos (of all shapes and sizes). One time I and my two corporals were on the footplate of a mighty engine from 7 pm – 1 am and at mid-night were taking shovelfuls of glowing embers and making toast. Toast, cheese and tea is awfully good at that hour!

That's it for now, I've a long day ahead of me tomorrow, especially as I happen to be in charge of the company at present!

---

12 Faygate was where Dad's grandparents had lived, near Horsham, Surrey. His grandfather had been the butler at a nearby stately home, Roffey Place. Faygate has a small station and it evidently reminded him of Dimapur, the railhead where all army supplies, munitions, tanks and troops were coming in ready for the coming battle.

Stories for the Future
20-12-43

I'm still really busy working in the open in all the hours of daylight and then at night writing official letters. Anyway, I'm as fit as I've ever been and am enjoying life a lot – I'll have more to tell you when I get home, in fact I think I'll take a few months holiday, we'll pension Dad off, get Mum a servant and won't send you [*Shirley, his sister*] to work until I've told you all my experiences – it's going to take years!

Christmas approaches
23.12.43

Today I've fixed enough 'wallop' to ensure a merry Christmas and I hear that the OC is also bringing enough to make it a 'tiddly' one – not a bad effort in the jungle!

Last night, in accordance with army tradition, the sergeants visited our mess (it is normally done on Christmas morning, but we wanted to ensure that we/they were sober when it came to us serving dinner to the men!). It was a hectic party and though I had a lot – (I held my booze – especially as I stuck to my own system of not mixing drinks) – I was delivering Sergeants home until the early hours.

Same letter – Christmas Day

Then came today – I awoke at 8 am and as it was the first rest I have had in a fortnight – I took my time getting up.

At 10 am this pup of mine was delivered by the locals that have befriended me and he is now settling in. Let me tell you about him – he is a Naga. They are hunting dogs, hill born, squat and massive and look just like small bears and hardly any ears, short stumpy legs – thoroughbred and very distinctive.

Mine is only 4 weeks old with a gleam in his eye which suggests a good dog to be. All black with a white band right round his neck, white shirt front, paws and white tip to his tail – a really good looker! I think I'll have to call him 'Slash' as I've now changed my truck which used to have that name and it will certainly suit him.

Our Christmas feast!

We have now had our Christmas feast, us officers and sergeants serving the men and it was a nice 'do'. Roast beef, spuds, tinned carrots, cauliflower,

Christmas pudding with rum sauce, mince pies, nuts, oranges, BEER!! – all out in the wilds!!

I seem to be soaking up mugs and bottles of wallop at regular intervals but seem to be holding up very well. Young Slash has had his share of grub too and now, after an exciting day viewing the great big world for the first time, is preparing to sleep it off.

I've had to do a bit of work this afternoon; tonight, I guess we'll have another bit of a party whilst the drinks last and then tomorrow we are back on the grind again – with a huge dose of work ready waiting for us.

JANUARY '44

2-01-44

The first letter of the New Year! Well, everything is going fine, our Christmas drink ration has at last been consumed; a couple of parties saw it off and we are now back on the job.

The whole period boiled down to a half day off on Xmas day. Today, Sunday, is the first break (another ½ day beginning at 3.30pm!) since then.

Nights in these parts are the time you can call your own, tho' the OC has twice said "We are invited to a party tonight" which to me is really an order: "You will come to a party with me tonight" – there's no ducking out, so last night I went to bed at 6 and rose at 8 this morning in an effort to make up lost sleep.

I haven't done so much travelling recently but instead have walked miles and in a small way have laid the foundations for a job for myself as Boro' Engineer, building anything, anywhere at any time.

The locals are a good crowd and every one of them smokes like a furnace – if when you meet them you hand round the 'cigs', not missing even toddlers of three and four, you are pals with them and they puff away most contentedly.

The censor- and troubled tales too

I'm almost in difficulties to know what to write about – I've so much of real interest which I mustn't say at present and little other 'copy'. Ian,[13] for instance, just returned from a six day 'job' sat down solid for 1 1/2 hours and poured out all his troubles – I still haven't heard the bright side and I guess we

---

13 Ian is one of two other Lieutenants in Company 589 with the same role as Dad. They both report to 'Syd' the Captain

could write a book a week with all the little incidents which occur and be sure of a 'best seller' every time!

Of course, I can now always fall back on Slash and Jai Lal, both doing very well and thriving, like me, on the present existence. Slash for instance now seems to take to a bit of training and follows me when I tell him and stays at home the other times. He can also find his way home from the cookhouse which may prove useful one day!

In two days' time I celebrate yet another anniversary – the third from the time when I crawled up a gangplank and sailed the seas – here's hoping that during this year I do the same again with a disembarkation port near home!

I own the company
12.01.44

At present I own the company, what is left here with me at any rate; quite a_pleasant job which, as you may guess provides plenty of opportunity for quick decisions and actions which, coupled with the fact that such decisions and actions can't afford to be wrong ones, is nice work if you can get it!

I've been exceptionally busy – therefore the time flies and I'm happy.

Now, as far as I can make out, we've broken the back of the work for a time and will be sitting back on our laurels, probably planting our kitchen gardens, to keep ourselves amused.

The 'off beat' Army look!
15-01-44

From the many papers you send me I see there is still plenty of Service Dress – Sam Browns and normal high-faluting correctness attached to the Army at home. Care to compare it with my existence?

On my last trip, me, 2 corporals, a sgt and a driver lived, ate and slept together for a fortnight. I passed out as washer up, Class 1 and a proven spud basher.

Since arriving I've done quite a bit of pick and shovel work, live in dungarees with a revolver and ammo slung around me and in odd moments during the last 3 days I've built a fireplace and chimney in the building which we are using as a mess.

Tonight, as the camp is mine alone, I thought I'd be daring and test my building skills – it works! But the wrong way – all the fire seems to be going up the chimney and the smoke is filling the room.

The 14ᵗʰ Army
23-01-44

The censor people have become tender hearted and lifted a ban!

You may now be told **that I'm in the 14th Army** – maybe so far you have heard very little or nothing of it but, believe me folks, you are going to hear plenty!

No doubt the ban is lifted to raise our morale a little – not that I've ever seen it weaken but there is still sometimes a tendency for people to think of themselves as a 'forgotten army'[14] when there are papers full of praise to every other fighting force in existence. Don't start getting worried tho', for you are as near to the Germans as I am to the little yellow baskets, so we are quits.

FEBRUARY '44

Whilst Dad was 'settling in' at Imphal and being kept 'oh so busy' the Japanese attacked **Arakan** *in early February,* 300 *miles to the West. 15ᵗʰ Corp held them, though the Japanese did make bold and dangerous inroads into Allied areas. After three weeks of intensive fighting the Allies recorded their first victory against the Japanese. Casualties at 5000 for Japan and 3500 for Allies were heavy but the news of this first victory was a huge morale booster for all – including those at Imphal.*

Preparations Continue
25-02–44

I've had a hell of a busy week since last writing – good though as it has been interesting.

By the time this arrives the papers may give you an indication as to what it is, and what has been happening – for now I'm saying nowt!

Today Slash has done 100 miles with me in the 'Mobile Sheep Dipper' as my truck is called. At one point the view in front looked darker than all the other surroundings and my driver asked me "Why?". I didn't know and we found out a few minutes later when we carved our way through a huge cloud of flies stretching about 50 yards. We had flies in the wagon for an hour after!

Another 100 miles on the road tomorrow, motorcycle this time. I'll add that all the roads except one are so dusty that it is like being in the desert. At the end of any journey eyes are tired, stinging and muddy with dirt. Also, that the mosquitoes are just starting their new season, fresh and full of all

---

14 Interesting phrase used, given that it wasn't made famous until much later by General Slim!

vitamins from A-Z. This area is a malaria 'hot-spot' so each evening we have a parade, and everyone daubs themselves with mosquito cream – it's just like being backstage in a theatre – it's a messy business but well worth the trouble!

Slash is growing fast! He seems fairly intelligent too, as he accepts some people as friends immediately but if others attempt to pet him, he turns, snarls and bites and generally scares them off. (He is quite popular with the troops as his chief adversary is the Sergeant Major!)

MARCH '4

The Japanese 15ᵗʰ Army crossed the Chindwin on the 8ᵗʰ March and headed with all due haste towards Imphal and Kohima. The Japanese plans relied on them defeating 4ᵗʰ Corp and seizing supplies before their communications and logistics broke down.

Quite A Week
9-03-44

I think I can say I've had quite a week. Last Saturday night I was wondering what clothes to take for a spell in hospital – a day of the squitters with a sign of blood convincing me that I had dysentery once again. Monday, I gave myself a dysentery starvation course and drank gallons of lime juice. On Tuesday I was so b**** y hungry that I had a big feast and since then I've been better than ever before – I'm cured!!

So much for health. I now regret to say that on Tuesday two of our ducks died – I'm not saying who chased them under a wagon, but I do know that duck, green peas and roast potatoes made a great change from bully – and later cold duck, more peas, lettuce and spring onions an even greater change!

Let me tell you how it happened – we left our last base with a structure built on top of Syd's wagon with bamboo and camouflage nets – inside 30 ducks and four chickens, with the 'gari' normal load causing it to groan under the strain. We arrived at our new location and took the ducks down to their new stretch of river. They liked it but did not know their way home; therefore, for the first few days Syd and I went to drive them home.

Alas!! One evening early this week they wouldn't come home so we threw stones beyond them to frighten them ashore. All missiles obtained their objective except one – I landed one in the middle of the bunch, just behind the ear of one unfortunate (if they have ears!).

His head went below the water and he drowned before we could apply artificial respiration.

A funeral pyre of green peas and roast spuds gave him a very touching send off and I'm now on a permanent duck collecting detail. The trouble is they are not our ducks to feed and cherish!

Orders for the Allied forward divisions to withdraw to Imphal were not given until 13th March. Imphal meanwhile had been left vulnerable to the Japanese 15th Division. With the Japanese in Arakan already defeated Slim was able to move the successful and hardened 5th Indian Division by air to the Central front – a highly successful move accomplished in just 11 days. It still left those already in Imphal somewhat exposed :

The Heat is On!
14-03-44

I'm afraid it's been a while since I last whipped off an epistle, but the truth of the matter is that I haven't done much other than eat, work and sleep – all in large doses.

We have been making history, the trouble is that the people haven't the time to realise the fact, so there are no bouquets to collect at present.

Actually, we felt rather hurt when a road cut from the mountain side collapsed under the weight of one of our wagons – onlookers merely walked away when they heard that there were no bodies to recover and a 400' drop hadn't left much vehicle to trouble about. Who was it that said, 'all in a day's work'?

Tension Rising
18th, 19th and 24th -03-44,

If things with you are in a state of tension that makes us quits, the only difference is that you do not know what is coming and we do.[15]

Things are rather hectic at present and some griff should appear in the news by the time this arrives. The Arakanders aren't doing so bad but this time I think we have even got them beat – anyway the historians can work it out I haven't time.

At present hands are swollen, nails ragged, blisters bubbling – active service at its best, digging deep and plenty. Still, don't worry yourselves on my

---

15 The day after this letter – on 19th March – the Japanese attacked Ukhrul, a town 30 miles behind Imphal. At that point it became obvious that the real target was Kohima, 60 miles north of Imphal, on the road leading up into the mountains and on into India proper.

account, I'm still quite away from anything and even if I wasn't, I wouldn't be more scared than anyone else!

19.03: Sorry I had to pack in yesterday, but the heat was turned on and I managed to get four hours sleep [*meaning 'I slept while we were under fire'?*]

24.03: I consider myself very young for the experience – I'm in a box. No, not that kind, the other one that's in the news and by jingo it's a strange experience. It may seem rather strange that I can even now write about such things, but the Japs already knows of our 'box systems', as long as he doesn't know where they are its OK. Hence my address (for this letter only – 'Troglodyte Terrace') as everyone of us sleeps in a hole dug by ourselves – the fact that mine is 71/2' x 51/2' x 3' may indicate how much I had to pick and shovel on my own little nook – a 3-ton lorry load!

Air above solid with planes

The air above us is solid with planes – ours – another thing that the little yellow baskets have discovered, and I've already stood the offer of drinks in Rangoon on Mid-summers day.

Our own job has been going on for some time – we deliver certain things to uncertain places [*i.e., tanks, troops and ammunition to the front line*], still are in fact, and guess who was surprised! Now we have had the honour to carry the first one of theirs [*i.e., the first captured Jap tanks*]: did I say we were making history!

Let 'em come!
31-03-44

Here we are again, full of the joys of spring and going well all round. Maybe you've seen some of the news from our way in the papers – first hand news from me – 'it's in the bag'!

I may be able to tell you more later but at present 'no can do'. None of us can ever have worked so hard before, nevertheless, now that the blisters have healed up there is something to look upon as achieved and we say 'let 'em come'!

Sleep has been the biggest snag just recently – getting up at 04.30 and going to bed when we can. I arose at that time on Tuesday morning, didn't get a wink that night, went to bed at 10 pm Weds and was awakened at midnight, next got on the charpoy 10 pm last night (Thurs) and had a really good night 'til 7 am this morning.

2 hours sleep in 66hrs wasn't good, but we survive! From tomorrow onwards it'll be 04.30 again.

APRIL '44

The Battle Continues
6-04-44

The Japanese began their attack on Kohima on the night of 4ᵗʰ April and quickly seized the dominating heights around the town. General Slim ordered a counter-offensive on 10ᵗʰ April. It took until 18ᵗʰ April for the Allies to break through to the Kohima garrison which, by then, was on its last stand.

No doubt you've been listening to the wireless and reading your papers like good citizens and maybe when the brain isn't too fagged, you've been wondering what the hell is happening out here and to the light of your eye in particular (see I'm not bashful)!

Well, here it is. Not news 'cause that's censorable but the old news as seen from the inside.

Jap has had it!

Before we go any further let me tell you that the Jap has 'had it' – is scuppered, b****ed, and any other way of describing it is ok.

He started off by making lots of the poor things walk a hell of a way and didn't give 'em too much grub to do it on – they walked at night and they always take the hard way by going over hills instead of round them, so's they could call the hill their own!

Alas, because distances are so great and there are so many hills, they have collected quite a lot for themselves – perfectly useless hills which don't even grow good grass!

Meantime, people like us stooge around in 'boxes', pop off now and again and kill the yellow baskets like flies: every time they try to get on the level ground the little babies which we tote around give'em hell!

Japs on three sides

Altogether from a spectator's point of view its extremely interesting – we've Japs on three sides, the main road to the outside world is our exit and that's all: we live just the same, eat just the same (and will go on eating OK for months and months and even if the grub should run low it's dropped like manna from heaven – good old RAF), drink wallop, write home and work just the same – and boy we've got some lovely guns.

Meantime the Japs are living on the land, living out in pouring rain, must be in a hard way for ammo and altogether I guess they wish they were a bit nearer to the cherry blossom and geisha girls.

I'll tell you a story – true!!

Two days ago, two of my boys were to collect some firewood in the Jungle; they walked into a clearing and a crowd of Japs walked in the other end.

The Nippons opened fire first but didn't hit anything, my blokes popped off with their stens, knocked over three and beat it in their wagon stopping a few bullets in the cab only. Score at half time 3-0! Just shows how easy they are if my blokes can hit 'em!

So – we are happy. Happier than before because this will speed things up a lot, we have not lacked anything, caught up on sleep, finished our digging and have some books to read on top of the daily SEAC. Just the job.

Income tax forms arrive!
13-04-44

Quite a bit of mail has arrived including the Income Tax quiz!

Imagine, here's us with Japs three miles away in one direction, being soothed to sleep each night by the comforting sound of our guns and some twerp manages to find a form which asks, "Do you reside abroad for the sake of your health?" and "Do you claim to be a British subject – if so on what grounds?", "Are you a member of a missionary society?"!

And how the hades do I know how much I earned in 41–42, 42–43 – the Army has never told me how much I have in 'credits' and I never had a clear idea of how much the Council were putting in the kitty.

Excuse me if I do not reply to them too soon!

News from this end of the war is very good – more and more Japs are finding honour, i.e., glorious death – either by their own hands or with a little bit of help from our lads.

Field hospital visit

The most interesting day this week as far as I was concerned was when I took a party to a field hospital as blood donors. Mine was not the type required or else I too would have 'had a basin' but we supplied the necessary and were on the job 7.30 am to 1.30 am.

At one o clock in the morning, I was watching operations being performed in the op. theatre and before that had helped a doc working on a badly battered chap who later passed out while still having a transfusion.

It so happened that I was on duty the next night (therefore not having any sleep at all) and so since then I've spent quite a time on my 'charpoy'!

Today I have travelled about 100 miles and now once again I've clicked on for duty and on the third stroke the time will be 0227 hrs precisely!

Convoys every day and a near scrape for Slash.
20-04-44

Although I have had a pleasant week the Japs around about cannot have enjoyed themselves in the least – they are still dying easily and fast and soon I guess will have to retire completely.

I have been running convoys everyday (we are naturally very busy) and thoroughly enjoying being away from my HQ Platoon.

One day we were out and had a few incidents to help fill our letters home. Slash as usual had accompanied me and sat gaily on top of the wagon.

While awaiting events at our destination he settled down for a quiet snooze between the rear sixteen wheels of the vehicle: it moved off!

Slash yelped, someone shouted, and the driver stopped dead. My pup was pinned to the ground by all the loose puppy skin on the top of his back and by reversing we got him out. He must take after me for luck!

A Jap attack

An hour after this little 'Slash' episode, the air became filled with the noise of planes. There are usually a number around (ours!) but this time it sounded like a real crowd.

Ack ack guns opened up and we ducked, lying on our backs to watch the fun. The Japs were so high that we never saw one in spite of the fact that it was a brilliant cloudless and sunny day.

A sudden crash and they had dropped their little lot about 1 ½ miles from where we were. It was quite a bang but unfortunately for them on top of a hill a long way from any people or habitation – what a waste!

The next day we read of it in the paper and learned that there had been 100+ planes, not all bombers of course but quite a crowd!

No repatriation

The other odd spot of dope wasn't so encouraging, especially under the present circumstances. The latest information re repatriation came round and gave the following enlightening facts:

- For BORs [*British Other Ranks*] – home after 5 years and chances of the time decreasing to 4 years.
- For British Service Officers 6 years
- For Indian Service Officers (i.e., Syd and me) never! with, for some time to come anyway, no chance of leave to England either!

Now can you see why we are in such a rush to get this business over – the only other alternative is to start a harem out here!

Heavy Japanese Losses
22-04.44

If you want a little more serious news from here-abouts – here it is. Pukka gen. The Japs are slowly realising they are up against it and so, in true Jap fashion, are dying off quite regularly.

So far, we have officially reported finding 5000 bodies. That, plus all those that are blown to bits, others that are buried, more just not found and, no doubt, large numbers wounded – certainly knocks a huge hole in the original force.

Such losses are irreplaceable as they are (a) operating miles from their bases in Burma, (b) lads of ours in the middle are tying up useful forces and (c) the reserves they need are not there anyway.

Truly Tojo is in the cart this time.

Prisoners are rare out here because the Jap is taught to commit hari kari rather than fall into enemy hands. Once a man has surrendered to the enemy, he is an outcast from Japan and so considers life not worth living anyway.

Up to date we have captured only about 30 – and guess what – they all had dysentery!

Air Displays!

For our own little bit, well – just now we are hardly more than spectators and very interesting it is too. Once or twice each day we have air raid warnings, but they rarely develop into anything.

As and when the planes approach this area, the Japs always find the reception committee waiting; the coloured lights and firecrackers are put up for their benefit and usually one or two stay for keeps.

The land side of things is rather better as we can see more clearly. This morning for instance, we were just going back to bed (we start at dawn and dusk and sleep when we can) when our guns, somewhere behind us, put up a beautiful little barrage. The shells went whizzing over our heads followed by the rush of air like baby rolls of thunder and fell plop on top of a hill some miles away.

I didn't stay awake to watch results as it's a quite regular occurrence, but I bet the poor devils on the receiving end did.

That goes on every day, usually when we are trying to kip down and, as and when our lads take over the hills previously fired upon, they always find plenty of dead 'uns to prove the accuracy of the gunners.

Another item that has been included in the daily program has been dive bombing demonstrations by the RAF and IAF (great competition).

These pilots take life very comfortably!! – They seem to rise late and do not start operations till 10–11 am. But when they do – O Boy …. We have a natty line of hills right out in front of us which have been feature No 1 for a couple of days and the lads have been laying their eggs exactly on the crest. We believe they are something to do with the 'Anti-Waste Campaign' as they crack the eggs on a knife edge and blow up the yellow bellies on both sides of the hill at once.

Strange I just mentioned dive-bombing parties – our lads have just staged another show for us – 3pm on a Sunday – they even let their lunch settle first!

Time for more sleep, no worries as we are enjoying things, just more mail please. So long.

Noises of battle now receding
27-04-44

As I told you earlier on, the Japs around here have 'had it'. The noises of battle are now receding as the Japs begin their trek back, still plenty of guns to listen to and dive-bombing to watch but all the noises are landing some way away these days – the nearest we ever had was about 2 ½ miles.

Its more than likely that our particular 'local' opponents will come back again as I understand that those which are left, after the mauling further up the road, are now coming to help them. You'll know by the time you receive this anyway!

If you have a large-scale map on which to follow the fun, you'll notice that everyone keeps making circles around everyone else – the fact that our circles are nice strong armoured ones allows us to squeeze the blighters in a way which they cannot hope to copy.

Latest report on a road where they've hurriedly retired 30 miles, says there is nothing left there but a horrible smell (dead bodies). Our lads found about 200 new ones but consider that very conservative as even 200 Nippons couldn't raise a whiff such as they found.

Now, the monsoon is just opening up: after several days of over-warm sunshine, we are just in the midst of a storm of large proportions with rain churning mud up like a cement mixer. This gives us another advantage as our roads are covered with tarmac and they have only mountain paths with rough bridges to cross what will soon be raging torrents. Same with airfields!

We are running in low gear at present – all the digging and road building completed and only the daily change around of 'salmon tins' to keep us on the go. I have made up all the lost sleep and more, though tonight I'm on duty again and will start bedding down around 5.30 am.

Talking of salmon tins, I'm afraid we give the Japs some nasty shocks sometimes – this whole affair is a case of playing dirty tricks against each other. Several times ours have met little salmon tins which pooped off a few rounds about turned at dusk and beat it like mad.

At dawn the next morning the 'rats' come tearing along to catch the 'retreating' enemy and meet some bloody great big 'tins' rumbling along the other way.

We must have been doing a bit of night work!

MAY '44

Easier times
4-05-44

It's been a smashing week all round. I've been round and about, had some mail, no over-strenuous work, tons of sleep and sunbathing and seen a flick. I'm on 'all night duty' tonight so I've tons of time in which to write and tons to say.

To start at the right end – last Friday I had a trip out on a road new to me but one which had been featuring in the news recently. We passed what had been battle fields a couple of days before and only at one spot saw any signs of Japs. That was where a party of them were marooned on a hilltop and our gunners were raising a fine show of smoke, dust and Nippons!

We went on and on, sten guns at the alert until we came across some of our customers – i.e., those we carry about. All the officers were too busy to worry about us – they were building a mess of bamboo way up yet another hill. The one or two not so engaged were sunbathing and described the situation as 'a tank man's ideal'!

Syd and I went out on Sunday morning to see if there were any Japs in a nearby village; a completely crazy idea I agree, but it was good fun for all that. Anyway, we only met some locals and then began a nature study.

This part of the world produces some very fine flowers (as well as snakes!), some English roses, honey-suckle and so on. I dug up an orchid and am now endeavouring to cultivate some more – what an optimist!

On Monday morning I gave a lot of my junglies some rifle practice, potting at empty tins across a river: some were quite good, others simply lousy but it was good fun and I managed to act the 'bura Sahib' by knocking over three in five shots. Needless to say, that afternoon was easily filled with rifle cleaning.

Tuesday bought the joyous news that we were to be visited by a mobile cinema; an Indian film booked for Weds and a British one for today, Thurs. I knew I was on duty tonight so Syd and I visited the IOR [*Indian Other Ranks*] show and understood half of it and considered that reasonable entertainment.

Tonight, Ian offered to stand in for me for a couple of hours whilst I saw an unexpurgated effort in our native tongue for the first time in 6 months. It was really great, Sonya Henie in *Wintertime*, seen on a good clear screen, with good sound production and us sitting on the ground beneath a quarter moon and tons of stars.

'Towny's Lucky Star'

Actually, today has been another super one. I was up at six and Ian and I took some customers out on yet another road where the fun is still going on. Naturally 'Towny's Lucky Star' came into operation as today was the first for some time that the road wasn't shelled.

As it happened, we sat back and watched our own lads push a lot of muck over instead.

Coming home I had a thirty-mile jangle in one of our wagons just to keep my hand in! Now I can say that although our little war is a battle for roads played out on the hills around them, I've travelled all the roads in question, and we've got all that matters while the Japs have only a lot more graves to dig (If they have time)!

Good luck continues
10-05-44

Once again, I'm using the all-night duty as a letter writing session – I've slept this afternoon and will turn in at 7 am so I lose nothing.

Here as always all is fine. I've had several trips this week, all to places which can't help being in the news: when we go places its always because something is about to happen or has happened and we are there to stop it. Anyway 'Towny' as usual took with him only good weather and no incidents – everyone says if the world was to end, I'd be up in an aeroplane and would miss it!

Generally, though, we are just that much nearer to clearing up this business. Every time our lads meet the Japs the rats come off far worse – their losses are many times greater than ours and all the incidents these days are of our choosing.

Syd, lucky man that he is, has left me to go to Poona for an interview. Meanwhile I'm left holding all the babies, good ones I admit but they are all mine!

CHAPTER 13

A Change from Tanks

16-05-44

I'm going to tell you about yesterday while it's still fresh in the upper storey, it was a day by no means normal in my sweet young life. Most writers, just to get atmosphere would say that "the day dawned bright and clear and birds chirruped etc etc". Not me! I give you the honest facts!

Yesterday didn't dawn at all, it just happened. When the bloke who was to call me at 5.15 am did call me at 5.15, I called him something – I also arose with the speed of a hearse and looked out of the basha door and saw atmosphere!

Clouds were floating around so low that you could reach up and touch them, those birds that were making the noise were all cursing with horrid shrieks, the general outlook was mud-covered, the ground was inches deep in mud too – it was also raining.

Sis Ram bowled up and together we filled the motorcycle tank with petrol, strapped on bundles 'til it looked like a Christmas tree, fed, gathered our two wagons and departed. With the usual 'Towny luck' as it is known, the rain stopped.

Roads like ice rinks

The roads were like ice rinks with their film of mud and Little Bo Peep's sheep had nothing on our trailers when it came to 'wagging their tails'.

I got a puncture on the way and let the two 'transporters' continue whilst I returned to base. At 8 am I was back in camp – whistled up a couple of lads and by 8.20 had swopped the rear wheel from another bike.

The sun came out – at 8.25 we set off again and covered the 30 miles to the supply depot by 9.30, with Sis Ram clinging on for dear life most of the way.

I arrived in the supply depot and what do I see – nothing, a mere nothing except one of my wagons towing another which had dropped one wheel over a 50' cliff! Another truck had come the other way and as our wagon had pulled out to give him space, the road had collapsed under the weight. It often happens and doesn't matter as long as the chap stops in time… ten minutes and he was out again!

I went to find someone who knew something and eventually found a chap who ran part of the place.

Said I, "I've come for 35 tons of Atta (coarse flour), where do I collect?"

"Um let me see, says he, that'll be 12 x 3 tonners you've got."

"No – only two lorries." Supply walla then looks me up and down checking for signs of insanity – apparently finding none, says – very s- l-o-w-l-y "But you can't get 35 tons on 2 lorries can you?"

I grasped him firmly by the arm to take him to have a look at the transporters – his jaw slowly went back into place!

A host of men sweated and toiled and piled sacks upward and sideways until they were tired. Atta went on, so did dul (a kind of chicken food eaten by Indians), cases of beans and jam.

A pause for a few bombs!

At 12 noon came an interlude, rather there came a whistle, a cloud of dust about half a mile away and a couple of seconds later a bang.

We were on the side of a hill and had a nice clear view of the plain below –the Japs, having carted shells all the way from Tokyo, now proceeded to aid our 'Grow More Food' campaign and for half an hour knocked hell out of the paddy fields which were waiting for a plough. All the lads had to do now was sow the seeds, the fields having been very neatly turned over.

As only one shell came nearer than the first, we considered the effort quite good entertainment and it helped fill the time till we tackled our bully sandwiches.

And what a trip back!

At 2.30 pm the loading was finished, tarpaulins tied down and we were away – down the hillside. A half a mile of bumping and seven sacks fell off and then we noticed that they had been stacked the wrong way, so that when we were straight, the load began to push itself off!

We tied, untied, re-tied, did everything we could to ease the situation but every few miles bags continued to fall off. I, on the bike, went behind with Sis Ram signalling the wagons if required to stop. It sounds easy but an 80lb bag of atta perched on the handlebars doesn't help the bike along: neither does a 96lb case of beans on the pillion!

A stop in a bazaar to purchase some potatoes and tomatoes and we continued. 6.30 pm, nearing our goal, I pushed on ahead to find the new depot. As an anti-monsoon measure the road had been 'made up' with stones the size of cricket balls. It was like riding on ice covered with marbles!

It was 7.30 pm and getting dark before I'd been four miles to the new depot, four miles back to my wagons on the main road, four miles back with everything to the depot – I had no lights!

Another host of 'cheery' souls were routed out to unload … 10 pm it was finished, lightning was all around us and thunder just beginning (strange but you can get each without the other here).

We pushed off, me leading in the light of the first wagons headlamp; after 3 miles I halted and waited for wagon No 2 – he did not come. Pitch darkness, heavy cloud, vivid flashes of lightning, twisty road and no lights – I went back to find No 2 and found him clean off the road, one wheel in a ditch and the whole caboodle as likely to tip on its side as not!!

We fiddled around in the dark for a bit, but it needed a breakdown lorry with a cable to hold it upright whilst another wagon towed it out, So back with tractor No 1 – now 10.45 pm.

From here the trip home was uneventful 'til reaching 'home' I turned into one of our own roads and so left the lights of the wagon behind me. It had to happen – I went straight into an entanglement of 'dannert' [barbed/razor wire] which some so and so had stretched across the track!!

After unloading our kit, I went and reported to the OC – that should have cheered him up at 11.15 pm – and no sooner had I got indoors than the heavens burst.

The rain was torrential, the thunder terrific, so much so that I didn't trouble to go outside to get my supper which had been left for me in another hut – but simply washed off as much atta, grease, dirt and mud as I could and dived straight under the mosquito net. That's all I remember!

At 3 am I was awakened by a tasty little barrage which some of our local guns were pumping out and at 8.30 am Sis Ram entered with some tea. But that was this morning and another day. Monday 15/5/44 was over – what a day!

As I said that lot was exceptional, even so it was good fun!! And 'all in a day's work' – nevertheless the boys say "One squadron of tanks rather than one load of Atta every-time!!"

CHAPTER 14

The Japanese in Retreat – we've Won!

22-05-44

The war (ours) has receded even further and the bangs and crashes of a few weeks ago are now only minor pops in the distance; very soon now the Japs will either pack in or be wiped out.

It's rather difficult for them I suppose as they mustn't be taken prisoner and to retreat without achieving their objective causes them to lose face and be no further use to the Empire – therefore they go on and on to the Great Beyond!

I've only been up to the 'front' once since I last wrote and as usual, picked an early closing day. It was completely quiet!

Burying them with bulldozers
28-05-44

When I tell you, a river rose 10 foot in a night, our bunkers, trenches and things like that became merely drainage ditches, people found their beds floating and a couple of buildings collapsed you may get some idea of the situation.

Roads became morasses and our wagons slipped off them without any effort at all – the Japs must be feeling it terribly as all their stuff has to come great distances by mule and elephant once they have managed to navigate the swollen Chindwin.

Anyhow plenty of the Nips have given up feeling about anything – affairs are at such a pitch that we are burying them with bulldozers!

I've been out several times in and between the rains but as usual I still miss the fun. One piece of road I went to was attacked 3 hours before we arrived and again 2 hours after we had gone. If you saw the place you would immediately have said, "what a lovely quiet spot – lets picnic here." So, we did!

JUNE '44

Victory in sight
3-06-44

The main battles for both Imphal and Kohima were now over – fighting continued in some areas until the end of July but for many – including tank transport – the work load for a while was less demanding.

To satisfy all doubts I'm fine but aching all over after an afternoon of football in mud & water, and everyone else is fine too – except the Japs.

Is it true what we hear about the new 'austerity knickers'? – one Yank & they're down!

I've been busy all week on planning ditches & culverts, doing a bit of digging myself too – our culverts have to take at least 15 tons – the weight on one set of wheels – so it's rather involved.

A mobile stage and recovery work:

Other strange jobs we have fallen for include turning two of our wagons into a mobile stage – we are now awaiting the arrival of a concert party to use it.

I really do not think there are many other jobs to which we can be put. To give you an idea of the forces we play about with – this is an extreme case:

A bulldozer was left in a river bed & the rain raised the water until it was almost submerged in the mud- shingle & sand built up against its side. We were told to pull it out!

It eventually came out – we used three of our wagons each with a 30 ton pull on its winch rope, each winch rope with a 5:1 ratio on blocks & tackle. 150 tons pull each, 450 tons!

Just to stop the trucks from pulling themselves backwards we anchored them by hitching each to a separate bull-dozer which kept running forward!

Nice work!!

I've now become a chess fan, so far I've never won a game but its very deep & interesting & most of our spare time is spent over a home-made board which I painted a couple of weeks back. You better start learning!

Plaudits for the RAF

The RAF are doing wonders – now, on top of delivering our grub, our mail & ammo etc, they are bringing back our lads who were on leave (BOR's).

Maybe, one day, even Jai Lal[16] * will be given a flip over the mountains. When he does I'm going to make him second driver on my truck (not now used owing to lack of petrol) 'cause Sis Ram as an orderly is too good to lose.

An Eight Foot Snake

Now for the SEAC Scandals of the week. First comes snakes, just to cheer you up. We've been chasing an eight footer recently <u>but</u> a couple of days back, when the boys were ditching, a Cobra sat up on its tail, puffed out its head & made nasty glassy eyes at them. Luckily someone swiped it in the back of the neck (about 2' from the top to be exact) & we're now building anti-snake traps in case the big 'un is a Cobra too!

Between you and me I coiled our catch up in a life-like manner and popped it onto the OC's 'IN' tray – the court martial date hasn't yet been fixed!

My sidelines

I've had a 'stay at home' week – building bridges, laying wire road, building a mobile stage for the 'Supremo' himself & fussing around my sidelines. Are you familiar with my side-lines – No. Well here are some of them:

- I'm Messing Officer which means I carry the can if rations turn up missing,
- I'm Offr I/C Photography – almost a sinecure as I withdrew all the cameras except the O/C's and mine – but we have no film!
- Acting Anti-Malaria Officer,
- Acting Intelligence & Security Offr,
- 'Secret' filer,
- Canteen Supervisor,
- Liaison Officer,
- O i/c all IOR's,
- water diviner,
- wood & wool gatherer & miracle man –

In fact, a general factotum. In fact, a nice job!

---

16 Jai Lal was Dad's previous batman. He left to go on leave several weeks ago and as we learn later never actually comes back. The reason – he had changed sides! He had joined the 'India National Army' which supported the Japanese. At this stage Dad was still thinking he was on a well earned break!

Aware of D-Day in Europe
9-06-44

Well, it's started [*referring to D Day on 6th June '44*] and for a time the 14th is willing to withdraw from the headlines while the local lads bash the Jerries for all they are worth.

No doubt everyone is as pleased as punch and I am sure that a lot of the recent tension has been removed. I'd really liked to have seen all there is to see – the colossal number of planes & mountains of equipment.[17] Still, if the lads hurry up we may see hundreds of planes where we now see dozens, just tell 'em so from me!

Our road almost open
21-06-44

We have been cut off from the wide, wide world for almost 3 months now. Anyway our lads are going great guns and our road[18] should be open in a few days to bring in more supplies and, so we kid ourselves, someone to relieve us while we refit. Even if our wagons are OK, I'm running out of clothes!

Some kind sole has introduced a rum ration twice a week and boy, oh boy, does it go down nice and warm. As it's meant to combat the damp I now move on to my next subject – the weather ….

According to the Gallop Poll of local BORs the weather in these climes is of one kind: ?*!!%& lousy. It can be hot & lousy, wet & lousy, or just plain lousy without any trimmings. Personally, I usually find it quite pleasant but for some time I've had to agree it is 'wet' and as a corollary its lousy too.

Our river has been playing tricks, it rises 20ft, drops 6ft, overflows its banks and the next morning is almost out of sight in the bottom of its own channel. Even so casualties have been evacuated in rubber boats locally so we might become marines at any time.

Last evening we had a pleasant 1.5 hours entertainment by Noel Coward supported by a single pianist. Together they put on a really good show on our mobile stage ---- it made quite a break.

---

17 Operation 'Overlord' had commenced on 5-06-44 when 1000 British bombers dropped 5000 tons of bombs on German gun batteries on the Normandy coast in preparation for D-Day.

18 This letter was written on 21st June. In the *Chronology of The Battle to Liberate Burma* by Edward M Young it states: "22 June: Troops from the 2nd Infantry Division, advancing from Kohima, make contact with troops of the 5th Indian Infantry Division coming up from Imphal. The Japanese Siege of Imphal is broken." This was a historic day for sure!

We've won!
29-06-44

Well folks, we've won!

Whatever happened on the second front earlier in the week passed almost unnoticed here. Our supply road was opened, wagons came rolling up, things went back to normal & the Jap attempt to invade India was squashed once & for all.

We are going to leave it to the historians to find out that it was our company which stopped the invasion – no transporters + no tanks: no tanks would have meant different results in several battles.[19]

Anyway, the first advantage has been that we have had a bottle of wallop apiece & can now recall the old flavour – 'bring more' is now the cry.

Of course our private war isn't finished by a long way – there are still enough yellow bellies around to keep us occupied for some time to come. They can't go home as we have cut most of their routes & even if they did they would have lost 'face' & maybe would have to kill themselves! Whatever next?

---

19 I've put this paragraph in larger text (it wasn't in the letter itself) as it seems so significant. Many of the officers in 589 Transporter Company had been through the same training as Dad and were recruited into the Indian Army at about the same time, some with him in Kakul. The Company was instrumental in getting equipment & supplies in the right place before this key battle had started and had now played an absolutely fundamental role in the Allies' success in both Kohima and Imphal. The Company had been split, with some, (Dad's pal Robbie and others) delivering Tanks at the Kohima end, whilst Capt Syd Hawes, Lt D A Townsend and Lt Ian (surname not known) played a key role at the Imphal end. It is amazing in such circumstances that the touch of humour is maintained throughout the letters. That does change in the coming months – but not before a well-earned leave!

CHAPTER 15

A Well-Earned Break

JULY '44

4-07-44

I've just had some super news – going on 10 days leave to Shillong on the 9th and flying out of this area. Whoopee!!!

Syd managed to fix it as there was only one vacancy in the brigade for a 'War weary officer' – as no one applied he bunged my name forward as I haven't had a break since January last year. It was accepted and fixed up today!

No doubt I'll be in charge of a party of BORs but I will only have to get them there and back – ten days to see shops and flicks, lie in bed and stuff myself with grub is worth that.

Our road now opened

Our long-lost Robbie, who I last saw in India and who, with his platoon, has been keeping the Company name at the other end of the road, has come up to see us and bring firsthand news of civilisation (at least 20 bottles of beer and noggins of Canadian Whisky!).

We have had tons of tales to swap and today has been a veritable old woman's session of scandal and experiences. Added to that our grub has improved tremendously too – today we had an egg issue, potatoes, fresh meat and other tasty items and the canteen stores have increased in variety – just the job!

One snag has been the recurrence of the rain after a few days bright spell. It makes us rather slack as seas of mud make work almost impossible. All the office stuff is rapidly brought up to date & all indoor jobs dealt with after which all we can do is to improve our chess, re-read our books or pick fleas out of Slash (a never ending pastime!)

Another company?

I've been thinking about applying for a posting to another company – not because I'm unhappy or anything, far from it, I like the job immensely but it was more with an eye to after the war when prospective bosses say, "What were you and where?"

There are jobs where having been an officer will count, but when people find out that one has been a lieutenant for years & years they imagine it is just because they weren't good enough for promotion. Such things as war establishments which lay down that there will be so many subalterns & other instructions which state that 'tank officers are to be recognised as specialists and are not to be posted from their units' won't mean a thing to blokes who want to run businesses.

Hence my current feeling. It won't be hurried & I've tons of time to sort the question over thoroughly & in any case I wouldn't like to leave my pals & platoon. Any ideas on the subject?

Leaving Tomorrow
8-07-44

Coo, I'm excited, just like a five-year-old who's purchased his first train set and can't wait to get home quick enough to play with it. Reason – I'm going on leave tomorrow, by air!

It all came about a bit sudden like but that doesn't matter at all, ten days in Shillong, roughly 14 days away from the company, is worth any amount of scramble.

So far only a couple of snags have struck me – we couldn't see one hundred feet on the hills today because of cloud, not too good to stooge around in a kite (note the rapid use of technical jargon!) and it so happens that the RAF don't bother to issue passengers with parachutes.

If my next letter comes to you written on a piece of cloud you'll know!!

I've used a little of my previous excellent (?) map reading training to gaze upon Shillong & find it is just 20 miles from the wettest place on earth – Cherrapungi – book out my submarine!

Civilisation is now going to be taken by storm; possibly it's just as well I'm not too self conscious or embarrassed when I do all the right things at the wrong time. Tell me, does one eat peas with the aid of a knife or a fork? Troglodyte!

A slight accident!

Graceful Gertie the Gliding Gladiator (me) did the neatest bit of riding on one ear witnessed in many a moon. I was jangling along through the sea of mud on a mo'bike when I hit a wave & suddenly wasn't!

Coming home on a wing & a prayer is about right. I was most certainly on one wing and if it wasn't prayers I was muttering maybe the local barbarians' blushes were caused by the wind.

You would have laughed, I know – I did myself later when I realised there wasn't one slightest scratch on me – just acres of mud. After hanging myself out to dry in the sun I was as good as new but slightly wiser

Shillong
16-07-44

It's that man again; well maybe not quite the same guy, as I now have to eat civilised and be a more 'refained' beast.

My leave has actually happened and I'm penning this from Shillong, two hundred miles from 'home'. All those things that we used to read about have come true.

I now climb up on to a bed instead of going down to it – one with real springs and a feather pillow; I wallow for hours like a miniature (please note) hippo in a bath big enough to stretch out in; food such as never was, comes in large doses – and often. Whew – did I say I was enjoying myself!

Have you ever flown? If you have, you'll know it's great, if not I'm telling you.

It was the first time I'd ever been 'up', and it was a grand experience. The trip over the mountains took only ¾ hour for the one fifty miles – we were lucky in having good weather with plenty of big billowy clouds and it was a super sight to look down on them in early morning sunlight.

I had a surprise when looking down on to the hill tops, I found they looked quite flat, all sense of rise was eliminated; however, they look quite normal and grand when seen obliquely and the trip was over all too quickly.

Huge areas of the plains have been flooded by the monsoon rains and being above them gave the impression of being on a cliff top and looking out over a muddy sea with islands popping up all over the place where the native villages were built up.

The rivers, some of them big 'uns, simply faded away into huge lakes and we could see roads and bridges washed away. Later on, a large lump of cloud pushed the plane down really low – over a solid jungle – and all my sins came up before me while I hoped the engines kept going!!

An eighty odd mile road trip followed, up from the plains to this place, a hill station at 5000' with plenty of pine trees (what a change from bamboo!) and often in the clouds itelf. It does make a pleasant change, and as I said, it's kind of civilized.

Strange though, I've yet to see a good-looking girl. Maybe I've been studying the flicks too much and am thinking in terms of Ann Sheridan and 'Oomph' but all I've seen around here have been old battle axes about fiftyish who soak up their liquor ration at a gulp and appear to scandalise about each other with perfect circular saw voices. Still, I'll wait – there's always England!

Walking for entertainment

Being in the hills and there being little petrol and fewer taxis, walking is the only means of stooging around. By some unknown means, everywhere is always miles from everywhere else and the daily mileage seems to be reaching astronomical figures.

I've worked out a system however – which includes lots of flicks, morning coffee and reading whilst reclining on the 'charpoy' and seem to be standing the strain fairly well.

The trip home should be good too. I've a sixty-mile trip down the other side of the hills, 150 miles in a train and then back along our own famous 'road' for 130 miles: still, that's in four days' time and I've plenty to do first. I'll let you know all about it next time….

A Turning Point in the war

The Battle of Imphal had lasted for four months and Dad's leave had been well earned. A chance for him to recharge and re-energise in preparation for what was to come.

The joint battles of Imphal and Kohima were a huge victory for the Allies but losses on both sides had been considerable. In all the Japanese suffered over 50,000 dead and casualties compared to around 16,500 for the Allies.

The fact that the Japanese supply lines had been sorely stretched had made a huge difference. The idea that the Japanese troops could 'live off the land' was a grave misjudgement and many Japanese died of malnutrition, starvation, exhaustion and disease as well as from the battles themselves. It was a hugely different battle to the one that Lt General Kawabe had expected when he set the initial expectation of three weeks to victory with his Japanese superiors.

The victory for the Allies was huge; this was the first major defeat for the Japanese and many have claimed that this was the true turning point in the Allies overall success against Axis, not just a turning point in the Battle for Burma. Had the Japanese succeeded in their attempt to 'breakthrough' to India then things could have been very, very different!

On 4ᵗʰ July '44 Japan's Southern Area Commander approved Kawabe's recommendation to abandon the Imphal offensive & withdraw back to Burma. The attempt to move into India had been quashed. A major victory for the Allies.

This was however not the end. This had been a victory on Indian soil. Burma was still in Japanese hands. Victory could not be claimed until major cities, such as Mandalay and Rangoon, were overcome. The move south to start in this endeavour is covered in the pages which follow.

PART 4

The Aftermath

August 1944 – February 1945

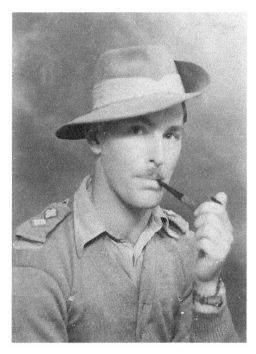

Lt D.A. Townsend. 14th Army 1944

CHAPTER 16

New Duties

July – August 1944

Back from leave – and reminiscing!!
24-07-44

I arrived back in the fold this evening.

The leave went from strength to strength: if you'd like that explained more fully it boils down to me and my buddies rolling from bed late in the morning to recline gracefully in a real bath, to return to the bed to cool down: thence to brekker; I still can't quite understand why the waiter bloke persisted in presenting us with a luncheon menu. Note that we are gaining 'strength' all the time!

Later a gentle stroll, not to any local beauty spot but anywhere downhill – return by the aid of a skilled thumb, waving in the right direction and nothing less than a staff car would do for our hitchhiking.

I wangled an extra day for all concerned and somehow took three days to do the two-day journey back as well, so for the while all are floating around in a sphere which' heeds not the common tasks of man' and the daily grind!

When I do come down to earth I may recall a few of the numerous jobs that the OC has 'offered' me. I'm going to be busy pal!

Glad to be in the Army!
27-07-44

Ooh, I've just knocked back a bottle of Canadian wallop and I'm feeling just fine. Whoopee! Honest, we are doing fine these days and it almost makes one glad to be in the Army – well almost!

On my return journey I called in at one of our platoons at the other end of 'the road'. My pal there is sitting pretty and is well known to all the hospital sisters. He took me round to their mess to tea – and I, for the first time in nine months, held converse with members of the fair sex.

I mean ordinary conversation for any length of time, not just saying 'Good Morning' to someone as I buy two annas worth of peanuts over a canteen counter.

I found it really great and as far as I can remember I didn't make any blunders – imagine me with my fingers crossed hoping against hope that I wouldn't come out with a bit of Army lingo!

Censorship

Your query on censorship is a bit ticklish to answer. Everything we see is strictly confidential and we never even discuss things amongst ourselves. However I can assure you it doesn't give anyone much pleasure in reading someone else's private business – and having suffered myself, it's even worse writing and knowing that someone is going to read it before it reaches its destination.

Now and again, someone brings out a wise-crack which doubles up the censor who immediately uses it as his own – normally though its sheer routine.

A second platoon to look after
29-07-44

Having once again settled down – I've taken over another platoon as well as my own as Ian has gone on leave – I'll try to answer some of your queries.

I haven't seen George since the flap began and I believe he now lives at the other end of the road. As Robbie, my pal who owns a platoon in the Coy is going on leave shortly I may take over his business too and then I should meet up with George as I'll just about 'live on the road'.

I'm looking forward to receiving the seeds and harmonica; both will be extremely useful in their own way, especially as, now we are not so busy moving tanks around, we organise two entertainment nights a week. Quizzes, talks, housey housey and the like all help to fill the evenings.

Tonight, we have a mock trial and the players have kept the whole show such a close secret that no one knows what to expect.

Secretary of State for War beware!

The day after I came back, I was given two hours' notice to give a talk! I gave the lads all the griff on 'leave and repatriation' and their feelings on the subject are very strong indeed – so are mine!

They also want to send a Ghurkha knife, very sharp, to Sir James Grigg [*the British Secretary of State for War*], who, in answer to nearly all questions states that 'his hands are tied' Maybe we can loosen them for him – anyway who ties them!

Meanwhile our war is over. The Japs are falling over themselves in their hurry home and are leaving tons of equipment behind them, including dozens of tanks. For a while at least our little show will be kept busy moving our customers around in small circles until all the tanks are back in their nests or back to the railway en route to war museums and 'Salute the Soldier' weeks.

Everything is back to normal as far as we are concerned – grub is plentiful again, so is petrol; the roar of lorries going passed has displaced the 'Bully Bombers' which supplied us for so long and is pleasant to the ears.

I find I know one of the chaps in the Air Supply and am going up in a supply dropping plane soon – just the job, eh!

'Slash' the pup has now finished doing cartwheels of delight celebrating my return. He's now back to his old stunt of howling down Vera Lynn records. Charlie Chan he loves – women wailing he does not!

He's a canny beast, this afternoon I prepared a bath for him, gave him a whistle and he doubled up in a smart soldier like manner; took one look at the water, turned about and disappeared for half an hour. A slip up on his part though, as he went in just the same and the water was cold by then – if he could have said all he was thinking – oooh – he'd have to be muzzled!

Bully bombing
31-07-44

I've been 'Bully Bombing' over the Japs – sit back and I'll tell you all about it.

Time – yesterday (Sunday) afternoon, 3 pm, weather fine but very cloudy; right foreground, RAF pilot suitably attired in PT shoes, short socks, thin shirt and shorts, horribly dirty and fitting where they touched, and an old bush hat rammed on at a rakish angle.

Enter from wings the hero – loud hisses – with sergeant in tow.

"OK for a flip in the kite" (speaks like a native this hero bloke) "we'll work our passage."

"Sure," says the RAF type 'we're not going far but it's very cloudy and we almost bought it twice this morning so it's up to you." Rapid translation of 'bought it' doesn't uplift morale much but we try anything once, so ups we climbs.

The plane was stacked with sacks and bundles with parachutes attached – there is no door just a big gap –ooh!! We went up a valley, between two ranges of hills and it wasn't too inspiring to see land above and below us as we bumped around in all directions.

Suddenly, as I look out 'the hole in the wall', all I could see was hills, stretching as far upwards as I could crane my neck – I thought we had come up against Everest or something but found that the plane was going round almost on one wing.

We found the lads who required the grub, perched right on the crest of a hill and as we flashed passed could see them wave – wounded and villagers staring up. The clouds were very low and as we circled, they disappeared from sight.

Inside, four of us worked like mad, piling bundles eight high in the gap, tying parachute cords to the wire 'trigger'. The clouds cleared, the buzzer sounded, and we pushed, hanging on for dear life so as not to follow the grub. The 'chutes opened and rather overshot the mark but near enough to be reached easily.

Next time round we were spot on; thereafter, things became rather hazy, we were 'flat out' piling, pushing, bumping all over the place – I know I fell over 4 times as the 'kite' hit air-pockets when I was lovingly caressing a sack of rice.

On one run up the hill we disappeared into cloud again and almost stood on our tail to avoid ramming into it. I kept my fingers crossed!

After 11 circuits we had dumped the lot and set back to look for Japs – in vain – they must all have been in their rabbit holes, but it was a wonderful sight all the same and the dose is going to be repeated often!

AUGUST '44

Carrying Jap 'salmon tins'
5-08-44

As I mentioned, I now 'own' another platoon, whilst one of the lads is away and am having plenty to do one way and another – they need a bit of shaking up!

I've been out on convoys a couple of times and am going to apply for a Jap Army Allowance as I've been carrying Jap 'salmon tins' – captured ones!

It makes a nice change anyway. Things are right back to normal, plenty of everything and now we are having all the Generals round to say "Thanks a lot." One came on Monday, another is due tomorrow but, as we have read their usual speech in the papers, it does not tend to mean much.

A whole day off!
7-08-44

There's no special reason for us being on top of the world at present but we are – everything is hunky dory. Maybe it's because the OC has gone away for a month.

I'm a bit mixed up on days and date at present – it's this-aways: another general fella came round yesterday, held a mighty big palaver, said "A fratefully good show, chaps, what!" heard two guns in the distance and went away.

To make sure that all of us 'boys' were around to kowtow and say our piece, the backroom boys said, "the 6th August will be a Monday and the 7th a Sunday – carry on normally on Tues 8th." It's confusing, whatever way you look at it so the great Towny, inspired as ever, worked it out that if August Bank Holiday Monday was a Sunday, he wasn't going to do much work!

That being the case all he had to do was creakily climb up on his soap box and announce that the merry men could have a complete day off! So great was the ovation that one chap nearly presented me with his rum ration, but a crafty look came into his eyes and he knocked it back in case temptation overcame him.

Heaven knows when we last had a whole day off – it must be just about a year ago – 'cause last Christmas we had to work all the afternoon preparing for a convoy leaving at 5 am on Boxing Day. Imagine the hangovers!

Collecting Jap tanks

I've been carrying Jap tanks around most of this week; things they have left behind in their haste to get back to the rising sun. Of course, these sardines may look all dainty like in war museums in the twenty first century and may even collect a spot of cash on show but why the blue blazes I have to cart them round beats me. Most of them are so small that they almost fall down between the wheels of our transporters and in any case, they don't stop our wagons from bouncing!

Hmm enough of this shop – a small concert party came round these parts and stayed with our company. Their normal show went down very well, but as our lads had given them a good welcome they put on a special 'off the headlines' blue show for us.

That's wrong, not quite for 'us' but for our boys – the sergeant major nearly went down on his knees saying 'dear, dear officers, please don't come'. The humiliation, to think that we can't laugh as long and as loud as the crowd, but even more, apparently, we were the butt for half the wise-cracks, and we couldn't even stage a comeback!

I've never heard so much jubilation before and not been able to muck in – hard done by, that's me.

Rain, rain and more rain
12-08-44

Coo, it happened this time – did I say we were having splendid weather last week? If so, cancel it!

For the last 3 days its rained even harder than before – our river is up 16 feet and has about another 8 feet to go before we start swimming for it! As far as we are concerned the weather is a greater enemy than the Japs ever were. Landslides and roads covered with mud causing skidding on mountain roads do nothing to prevent the grey hairs! I know, 'cause I skiddied and boy oh boy, did the long drop look dark and deep!

I've been out a couple of times during the week; when I say out, I mean trips of a hundred miles upwards. Yesterday's was 170 miles and I started at 6.30 am to arrive home again at 10 pm, with a halt of four hours whilst the road was cleared by bulldozers. A great life this but the odd Guinness or two would make it a whole lot better.

Bodies Everywhere – first aid needed!
16-08-44

Twas last Sunday eve, I and a pal, entitled Syd, were jangling along in a truck bound for nowhere in particular when we rounded a bend – and there it was.

A wagon was on its side, bodies were strewn all over the road, under the wagon, on top of each other, spare pieces, odd arms and ears were lying around just waiting to be matched up. Coo, I've never seen so much blood and bone going spare outside of a butcher's shop.

Silent, Syd and I got stuck in and endeavoured to clear up the mess; I first concentrated on a bloke (they were all locals, Manipuri) who had his thigh bone sticking out just above his kneecap, amongst other things. Another one was already glassy eyed while the rest were feeling exceedingly sorry for themselves.

Someone produced a first aid box and we dished out morphine to those in need – no one present knew any more about first aid than we did so we just carried on! Eventually we fixed up all the bodies, eleven of 'em, into ambulances and pushed off to the nearby river for a wash down.

That wasn't the end of it! As we were washing, a huge lizard or young Alligator walked just about 10' in front of us and the fearless Syd shot it absolutely dead with his six gun – he has already put in for a posting to Hollywood, although he realises, he could never hit a haystack at 10' in future.

I spent Monday morning in skinning the creature and morbidly devouring the news that three of our previous day's customers had gone beyond the Great Divide.

More bully bombing

The American Pilot who took me on this week's air trip came out with a cheering line of:

"Waal I'd better not make the drop, 'cause we'd never get back in time to miss that there staarm [*storm*]; in fact I doubt if we all would get back at all! Mebbe we could land the kite at 'A' – (200 miles away!!) but it's a lousy base- it doesn't have any booze."

Ooh me nerves isn't what they used to be.

We were carrying a load of petrol, cordite, grenades and ammo about the clouds and took it up and landed twice in efforts to go through the thunderstorms – I'm going to stick to submarines in future.

CHAPTER 17

Convoys and Jap Flags

September '44

24-08-44

I've tons to write about again as I've been away on a job for about a week.

Naturally I didn't keep up with the news and now I find the map of Europe has completely changed: Paris and Marseille liberated, our troops swarming all over France, the Russians banging away as hard as ever, Romania packed in- and even out here our lads have been hard pushed to keep up with the Japs advance <u>out of</u> North Burma!

I suppose and hope that soon the Calais coast will be cleared and with that the flying bomb business should be considerably reduced – and no one will be sorry![20]

The Latest Trip

Now to tell you about this trip of mine – it was great, from start to finish as I had a large convoy of wagons all to myself and could tell everyone and anyone just where they got off. So many people try to boss us around, but we say:

"You don't know what you are talking about, our trucks are twice as heavy as anything else you can produce, and we know just what they'll do!"

I drove a considerable distance myself and now have an even greater opinion of our lads. To go technical, we have two gear boxes, 12 forward gears and three reverse which of course makes things a bit complicated. I've had to change gear ten times in a hundred yards more than once and from top to bottom in ten yards often! In fact, I ended up with a big blister in my hand with the drivers saying "Ya soft!"

---

20 letters received as well as the 'SEAC Times' kept those in Burma surprisingly well informed of the overall war's progress

Travelling all day on windy, hilly roads with blazing sun and super scenery was worth the trip alone, but when, on arrival I met Robbie and he said that we were going to a show produced by the sisters whom I met previously I thought things were really fine.

Actually, the show was 'not so good' – we told them so and also suggested how it could be improved and eventually were incorporated as 'Critics in Chief'.

Anyway, we were well 'in' at the Sisters Mess, entertained to tea the three days I was there, dinner one night, dance on another and we had a foursome picnic last Saturday afternoon. Oh boy, those girls did us well, they were a really nice crowd with none of the usual 'nose in the air' attitude that is common out here and made us feel at home.

In return we provided our trucks to take them to the Garrison theatre each evening and I think that 'Towny's Taxi Service' became a local feature! To sooth everybody Robbie and I saw the show on its third night, and it had improved out of all recognition – we said, "We told you so – and we'll do the same again anytime."

And this is what a convoy is like!

_Now I must tell you all about my convoy – you've never been on one, have you? OK, you can come as a passenger.

We awaken early, mutter a silent prayer that all the wagons will start and jingle off down the road. Halting neatly in bundles of three we wait while our customers [*i.e., the tanks*] rumble down the road, climb aboard and are securely anchored.

The highlight of all convoys is the number of brews of 'char' that appear, and it is only with great difficulty that our clients are restrained from brewing up before we even move.

Towny makes mystic passes with his hands and all his wagons begin to move – except two! He later finds that these thugs each collected a puncture in the first mile and were having wheels changed; you see how fussy my lads are, they've still thirty-three wheels on the road but must have the final one!

Dozens of vehicles become stuck behind the convoy unable to pass on the narrow roads and we carry on unperturbed at a steady 3-10 mph as we climb the mountains! At mid-day we meet the cook's lorry (sent on ahead) and dig into a good meal, plus char, whilst about four miles of trucks, all shapes and sizes go past head to tail with the drivers all muttering dire things. Can't understand what upsets 'em!

By the time they are gone we are ready to move again and continue the funeral march. There is only one spot where we can stop for the night and we arrive at dusk after having unloaded and re-loaded at a bridge that looks as though it were made of mecano – much to the disgust of the new heterogeneous (good word that!) collection behind us.

Just about to settle down for the night Towny decides to count his wagons to find that ONE IS MISSING. Coo – he is annoyed and goes back in his truck to find it. A ten tonner has rammed it and suffered a fate worse than death, even his wagon has come to a standstill. Eventually all is collected and a good night's sleep, by the roadside under the stars ensues.

Next morning, we move off again, nearly all downhill this time and brakes become red hot and catch fire, wheels fall off, and tyres burst (nothing very serious). We arrive in the afternoon, the tank wallahs mop their brows and tear off as if they are glad to leave us. We then settle down, again by the roadside to three days of repairs, refuelling, re-loading and light entertainment.

Two days to go 'home' again are very much like the outward trip – now I'm told that I'm to leave again in four days' time. Guess this life is going a bit too fast for me! I'll be back with the next edition as soon as I can but cannot say from where it will come. Keep hoping, will you?

SEPTEMBER '44

Collecting Jap tanks – and an unusual flag
04-09-44 (11 days later)

Before you tear a strip off me – let me explain [*the delay in writing*]. Towny has been working again – yes really. I arrived 'home' last night after being away for 8 days, eight rainy, dismal, hectic, hilarious, smashing days – we mix our business with pleasure!

It was a good one again in spite of wicked weather – it rained every day and night and although I have a tent arrangement on the side of the truck everything got wet and most of my kit dyed a dirty red with camouflage paint!

Now – to satisfy your desire for news and scandal from the East:

Well, as and when you see a Jap tank you can say I know all about them and just who brought them back to civilisation. And had you seen it you would have laughed and laughed! The tanks were knocked about rather badly so, to avoid our lads thinking they were ours and becoming despondent, I made a 'Jap' flag!

A pair of Towny Pyjamas, light blue, unserviceable, Mk1 were ripped into a rough rectangle and daubed with a brilliant red circle.

Odd hieroglyphics were added which looked as much like Jap as anything else and all was set – we flew the creation at the head of the convoy and simply dozens of people offered my drivers fabulous sums for the thing!

I've discovered an easy way to make a fortune now, but I've run out of old pyjamas – any ideas?'

Slippery roads

Coming home again should have put years on me – but didn't. The road was like an ice rink as far as we were concerned and the leading vehicle (me on it!) had to find the difficult parts. And we did!

Lots of times the whole thing slipped sideways on banked bends and once the weight of the trailer on a steep hill just jack-knifed. I, lucky as usual, rammed the cliff face instead of turning the other way and going over a 700' cliff – it's all part of the fun!

Two weeks ago, it was strongly rumoured that we were going back to India for a break – now it is fairly certain we won't. I'm not sorry as in a way its best to be in the midst of things (well just behind)!

Convoys over for a while
9-09-44

I've once again settled down to a peaceful life of stagnation; convoys are finished for a time and home comforts are all working smoothly. I can now sit back, feet on the desk (well between us the desk is an old bully beef box) and dream of iced sundaes under multi-coloured sunshades on esplanades anywhere and everywhere.

Maybe I'm painting the wrong picture though. The old man has been inspired and everyone does half an hours' PT each morning which is an exceedingly bad way to start a day.

Attempt to cross the Chindwin

Because the weather had improved and our lads had advanced so rapidly, I took an afternoon off last Wednesday in a crafty attempt to fly over the Chindwin.

Darn my hide, I was misled; my plane did a sharp right turn at the air traffic lights and ended up flying round in tight circles over three huts which were at least twenty miles from the nearest Jeep track. Mind you, I don't blame the lads down below as they had to walk – and you should have seen the mountains – but the chap who sent them there must have been crazy or hadn't someone told him the Japs have gone home.

The flight was once again super in spite of having a madman at the controls: coming home he came down to about 10' over the plain and had to lift the machine over villages and trees.

Hiking bug!

I'm afraid the hiking bug has bitten me too – today a pal and I crawled up a 500' ft hill just for fun. When we had recovered and dried our shirts in the sun, we found the view to be worth the effort. Can you wonder that my chief post-war aim is to have a bed with a feather mattress at least a foot thick?

Well, it looks as if Hitler has had it and all our boys will be coming out of here toute suit – will you let 'em know that we will have the flags out for them and will lay on a special 'bully 'feast – the lucky people.[21] *

September continues to be quiet.
23-09-44

It's been a very uneventful period here recently, so I haven't any 'griff'; constant rain, acres of mud and low clouds have kept me 'grounded' this week and we haven't given the lads 'up the front' any grub from the air.

All this is very soon going to change once again!

---

21   Interesting that although 'peace' was still a year away, there was a feeling, at least within the Imphal based troops, that it could all be over much sooner.

CHAPTER 18

Down the Tamu Road

October – December '44

OCTOBER '44

Operation Capital

On 16th September '44 the Combined Chiefs of Staff had approved operation 'Capital', put forward by Lt General William Slim. This was the overland advance into Burma.

Quoting from Edward M Young's ' Meiktila 1945: The Battle to Liberate Burma:

"In anticipation of operation 'Capital' Slim had kept his forces pushing hard against the retreating Japanese despite the onset of the monsoon, which turned small streams into rushing torrents and jungle tracks into rivers of mud.

By early August the Imphal plain had been cleared of all Japanese forces. Slim ordered the advance across a broad front to give the Japanese no time to regroup. The 14th Army's objective was the Chindwin River."

The crossing would not be achieved until December. Meanwhile as you will now read convoys were back in action, moving tanks, equipment and supplies towards their objective.

Though there is no detail on Dad changing Companies, his address is changed from 589 Company, RASC, SEAC to 64 Company, RIASC (Corps Transport), SEAC. We learn later that this Company is supporting the move to the south, down the Tamu road. It is very definitely in the thick of things – read on!

Convoys everywhere – at speed!
23-10-44

Cor, luvaduck, I've had it, I've bought it, I don't know if I'm coming, going or gone, whether I'm travelling in right hand or left-hand spirals; in fact I'm not sure that I should sit down to write this – standing up or a prone position would be equally suitable.

Allow me to expand upon the subject – Towny's travels are increasing at a speed which is almost leaving him behind, he's here, he's there and everywhere, all at the same time.

It's like this 'ere: things were all fairly normal up to last Thursday – 19th; by normal I mean that all that happened was that I shifted my platoon [*40 + vehicles + men*] to a new spot, built cookhouses and dug all the holes that go with the camping and on one hectic night attended an Indian bust up put on by my lads. It consisted mainly of rum, curry and goat, duck, sketches in Urdu and some of the most bloody awful singing I've ever had the mis-fortune to hear!

Well, I survived the week until 2 pm Thursday, then all hell opened up and showed me just what life in the raw could be like. I think you've an idea of where I live. Willy nilly, I was told to take my boys to a place 50 miles away, to be prepared to live there for two months, to be there by 7 pm that night and to start work next morning.

OK, OK, things like that can be done – my tents and cookhouse were all knocked down again and we were there at 7 pm. Things had gone too well though and the back room boys had everything worked out.

Leave 10 lorries here they said and take the rest 30 miles down the road (what a lovely road!). Even that was done but to further ease the situation they split my 30 remaining wagons into groups of 10 and parked them 2 miles apart! All I had to do was to feed the host, fill 'em up with petrol and be ready to move off at 6 in the morning!

We settled down at midnight after a final shaft of "The job will only last for one day and you can go home on Saturday."

That did actually occur and by the time I got home on Saturday night I'd covered 350 miles since starting.

Bed early on Saturday after flinging up tents again seemed really too good to be true – and it was! At 10 o'clock yesterday (Sunday) morning came the dope "Leave at 2pm for a fortnight at the place you left yesterday."

Loads of sympathy please – we've made it, the tents are up, the holes are being dug, all except three of my wagons are out on the job and I'm now attempting recovery. The mileage since H hour on D Day stands at 524; poor old Slash is tender all over and simply can't make up his mind whether to sit down, lie down or just die. Anyway, I'll let you have further griff when we both recover.

NOVEMBER '44

October had evidently been pretty hectic. To put this into perspective a quote from E M Young Meiktila 1945: The Battle to Liberate Burma *once again:*

"14ᵗʰ Army divisions fought their way down the Tamu and Tiddim roads against the Japanese rearguards, which even in their weakened state fought desperately to cover their retreat."

Tanks and all other supplies would have been taken down both roads,with Dad's Company focussing on Tamu. Having delivered to the required destination, by 9ᵗʰ November (the letter below) Dad was back in Imphal. The cargo he had left behind was very successful, E M Young continuing:

On 14ᵗʰ November the town of Kalemyo was found abandoned and, on 2ⁿᵈ December Kalewa, on the Chindwin was captured.

Slash the only newsworthy item
9 -11-44
I'm home again and on the way back called in at 589 to view Slash's family. The boy didn't know his own strength, fathered seven at a go! Panda's rather than puppies – just like Pa was and the lad's way way back are bidding fantastic prices for them.

Well, I don't seem to have included much of my own news mebbe next time![22]

South of the border to Tamu
19-11-44
Late again I'm afraid but the wheels have to keep rolling which seems to keep me away from 'home'. Latest effort was to go south of the border as far as Tamu – and boy, what a road. The dust is worse than any I've previously met. Now I've been to Burma on the ground as well as in the air, so I can chalk it off as yet another country visited.

---

22 Remember that the censor had to be observed. Interesting as ever that although he had recently dropped off tanks and troops prior to their success at Kalewa 'Slash' was his only news!

I met Syd and Robbie from 589 on the road several times (splitting the odd tin of bully and sharing 'a mug of char' with them and of course I pulled their legs about their bl**dy great wagons blocking the road for people who have a job to do (i.e., me!)

I'm off again in the morning so now I have to pack up the odd bits and pieces necessary for a 200-mile trip in two days – I assure you there's not too much baggage. It's mainly washing kit and a couple of tins of grub for Slash – he won't be left behind!

Tiredness takes its toll
22-11-44

Maybe I had better tell you of recent happenings to fill in the story – as I guess it sounds crazy just to step off a cliff!

On Monday 19.11 I and my boys pushed off in another convoy, drove till 4 pm, were loading mules until 9 pm, fed and sat round fires 'til 1am (20/11) and then started on a great trek – at funeral speed (average 7mph).

I always run at the rear of my convoys to repair all the breakdowns, so knowing that all our flock is in front of me (they couldn't really get lost as there is only one road!). We jangled on through the night – then through the day and at 7pm were still 20 miles from our destination.

After 18 hours on the road after a night without sleep, everyone was rather drowsy. Point No 1 – 'cause I was too! Yet another of my ancient steeds gave up the ghost and after a spot of basic English and hefty spanner work, I brought it back to life – using up my torch battery in the meantime!

What little moonlight there was, threw the most deceptive shadows and, as I walked back to my jeep, which I'd parked 6ft from the edge of the drop, I was thinking more of food, sleep and roaring fires – than anything else.

It just happened that between me and the jeep the rain of ages had worn back the cliff edge right to the road. So, Ten Ton Towny, aiming himself at his jeep headlights nearby – took an almighty high dive!

Oh, by the way we finished driving at 11 pm – 150 miles in 22 hours – and could almost have walked it as quickly!

It looks as if I'm going to spend Christmas in Burma this year – which kind of assists the 'East – ever Eastwards' plan. To date Army Christmas's have worked like this for me:

South Wales 1940, Cairo 1941, Kashmir 1942, Manipur Jungle 1943, – which isn't a bad slice of world touring.

Back 'home' again – a feast
27-11-44.

Today is a Mohammedan feast day, equivalent to our Christmas, so everything is running in bottom gear while the boyos ooze around with their shirt tails dangling and towels wrapped round their heads. Towny, believe it or not, is not squatting cross legged on the floor (yet!) but is writing this in the approved manner, chewing his fountain pen into a tasty paste.

'Tis only 9.30am so I reckon I deserve a medal for my speedy start and good intention – however, even our workshop has closed down so no medals can be minted today. At 12.30 I'm due to go along to help polish off the fatted calf (?goat?); possibly then I'll have to sink on my haunches but as the OC is rather a big man, I've a feeling that even then we'll have a table provided.

3pm – I'm recovering slowly chum, the lads have done their durndest to scuttle us and only the fittest survived. It was more of a passive Indian Mutiny than a normal meal. This is how it went:

Act 1 – Trooping of the Officers

Officers troop to where their loving men are squatting on the ground in rows, stuffing themselves with eeeeenormous quantities of rice and goat; piggily watching two other sepoys, stripped but for loincloths, wrestling with each other with a sheer dis-regard to the damage caused to the earth as one threw the other away.

I gathered the impression that all the food was finished and these two had been told "If you want any grub, eat him!"

Officers then troop to the mess and without using the sextant, decide the sun is down (1200 hrs!) and it's time for Gins. Gins it is.

Officers then troop to the Thatched Hut where, watched by VCOs [*Viceroys Commission Officers – roughly Sergeant Majors*] and Havildaro [*Sergeants*] they subsided into groaning seats.

Act 2 – The Feast

A scurry of feet and Towny, turning from a spot of conversation with his neighbour (Bless his Mohammedan Bed Socks) finds himself confronted with a plate piled high with rice, with great knobs of meat sticking out all over the place.

Towny smacks his chops but suddenly remembers that he's an 'Officer and a Gent' and grabs the plate and shoves it in front of Hussain Khan.

That makes things rather awkward as ole Hussy has already one in front of him and it slowly dawns on T that the reputation of the British Raj has descended upon his shoulders: he's got to eat the lot or bust in the attempt. He also realises that several other people round the table have seen the light too – each of us could feed the multitude with his own plateful.

Just as T is squaring his shoulders and surreptitiously slipping his belt three notches in anticipation, a dark hand shoots over his right shoulder and whams a cold roast duck on the table in a way which rattles all the glasses (empty!).

Some bright spark notices the void in said glasses so brims them up with rum, looking sorry for the while, as if he's apologising for the fact that there aren't two glasses a piece.

There's no end to it – more ducks arrive, plates of curried maybes and has-beens and piles of chapatis – which goes for bread in these parts – like unleavened bread – depth charges! If someone had shouted "Seconds Out" and a gong had sounded I would not have been the least surprised.

There was a sudden swoosh, and everyone shot one arm forward and got a firm grasp on some extremity of duck. They seemed to work out at one duck between two, no knives or forks, nothing barred!

Mohammed Hakim and I came to terms and he neatly burst ours into two, presenting me with the wishbone half as if he were bestowing on me the Grand Order of the Companion of the Bath (with the plug pulled out).

Thereafter it was every man for himself, the only weapons allowed were spoons for churning the rice. As far as I can recall the only thing that didn't happen was that for once used bones were not thrown over the shoulder after completing the gnawing process – they were merely put in a neat pile in the middle.

I was rather groggy by the tenth and last round but finished up with a win on points – the backbone of the British Empire is now supplemented by an unfinished wishbone and the Sahibs are 'orribly tired'.

Act 3 – The Speeches

Arise the Major "Bravo, Jolly fine show. Thanks!" (in Urdu) "Whew!!" (In English). Subsidence of the Major

2nd i/c "Nice going lads, the best meal ever, Hick!!"

VCO replying "Hrmph! It gives me great pleasure to welcome the Sahibs (Wah!) to our feast. May their lives be long ones. Ourmh!"

Towny sits quiet on the thought that if there was another cliff handy, he'd jump over it! (I've now completely recovered from the high dive!)

It's over, the bulk of the people around here are sleeping it off – I couldn't sleep if I tried – and it should now remain somewhat normal till Christmas.

DECEMBER '44

Christmas greetings

Aren't these things twee? *(see pictures in appendix)* I've had them for months and only by imposing the greatest restraint upon myself did I postpone sending this till now. Somehow it didn't seem right that it should arrive by Guy Fawkes Day, which it certainly would have had I posted it on the official 'mails for Christmas' date. So – hoping that this arrives about the appropriate time I duly send you bags and bags of special Towny Christmas Greetings, good luck, health – yes and even wealth – and of course happiness.

You don't have to worry about Towny over the Christmas period – ever. He's now saving up like mad to pay for his booze ration and he has never yet failed to recover by New Year's Day – but New Year's night – oh boy oh boy!!

These funny signs dotted round this letter may keep you guessing as much as they do me. Top left is the phoenix of the SEAC badge: bottom right is that of the 14th Army – the others I consider beautiful too but haven't the slightest idea what they represent.

And more anniversaries

Do you realise that we'll soon be celebrating an anniversary – the day you first wrote to start all this mutual mud – slinging; you've got to admit though that it's been good fun, so keep it up!

At roughly the same time, 4th Jan, I'll be commemorating the time I tripped over the gang plank in Liverpool – four blessed years, a baby lifetime.

Still, while I think of you receiving this in the cold, damp, maybe foggy day, you can cheer yourself with the thought that at least our weather is nice – just like a sunny morning in May, birds singing, butterflies flapping and Indians shivering.

It's really the sort of day that one should bash the old Austin Seven into the country and leaving it under the trees, take the picnic basket down beside the river amongst the grasshoppers. Things to Come!

A trip to the Front‼
15-12-44

I'm on the first day of a six-day convoy to the Japs and back and as you can see from the address, I'm at the 'Dusty Wayside', awaiting the wagons to be loaded.

Interlude – to continue – - do you mind putting my name forward for a KCB or somphin' in the New Year's Honours list!

I had to take loads and loads and loads of hooch, whisky, sherry, brandy and beer – miles and miles and miles to the forward lads for Xmas consumption and it all arrived!

(My OC has just unlocked the handcuffs.)

Actually, it nearly didn't arrive 'cause I went so far that I saw a lot of people waving little red flags – I didn't trouble to wave back. Did I tell you that my jeep holds the speed record for reverse gear!'

CHAPTER 19

Training New Tank Transporter Drivers

January – February '45

Driving and Maintenance School – Shillong
31-12-44

Lt D.A. Townsend, RIASC, 202 Area, D and M School, L and C Command, SEAC[23]

Here's what you have been waiting for folks, the Christmas carol and the new address all in one lump. I have arrived here, Driving and Maintenance School, today after knocking off 580 miles of road travel in four days – more about that later.

Christmas was completely up to expectations, grub and etcs perfect – in fact I got more than I expected as I was out on convoy all day on the 24th and didn't reach the Company until 0600 Christmas day – but the night!!!

By some means or other all the officers of 64, who had been scattered over 600 miles of land three days previously, all managed to 'home-in' in time for a grand bust up – we eventually did bust things, but no one was worried. One chap came from Calcutta by air with 400lbs of 'kit' (normal allowance 40lbs) and the other 6 cases are on route by road – thank the Lord that America repealed prohibition!

The next day (late) I finished my odd items of packing and buzzed off up the road to collect a lorry and a 'party' which I was to bring here – and spent the night in another company who had just received a turkey for their rations (we'd seen off two 'home reared' geese the previous night!).

---

23 Note re 'L and C Command' – this was officially formed a month before on 15th November '44 under General Sir George Gifford. Responsibility was for 'Lines of Communication' – supply routes to advanced bases, Assam Railways, vehicle replacement, changes in supply lines etc., etc. The driving training school was therefore a temporary move away from the front line.

On the morning of the 27th I set off feeling as though I never wanted to eat again and by 3 pm had travelled far enough to clear the bad, dusty and bumpy road. As always, there was a snag – an enforced halt of 5 hours rather upset the schedule and we didn't arrive at the nights rest place until 1 am.

To fit in the next day's mileage, we had to leave at 6.30 am so I began to wonder if, among all the pills we take, some sleeping pills could be included.

Breakfast at 589

Anyway, I called in at 589 for breakfast to cheer the lads on. While I went back, I saw two of Slash's pups – rather like Dad they are but not quite so bandy. I still think he is an original.

Everyone was recovering from a period of celebration – they were very hazy about what they had been celebrating – but were looking forward to seeing me somewhere south of Mandalay when I go back.

Two more days of travel on the road followed. Yesterday we knocked off 231 miles in 11 hours and today did only about 70 miles – all up hills. It's been very interesting seeing the changes from mountains to plains and back to mountains; from jungle to paddy fields back to cultivated palms and bananas – then more jungle and finally pine forests.

Slash at one point went Monkey chasing – here he has to run around to keep warm.

So – back in Shillong!!

I've already settled in and boy it looks good. I've a bungalow to myself, bags of room and not much furniture; a roaring fire …… only two other chaps and myself to run the school and a cook to feed us who came from the hotel I stayed at when I was last here.

Now I'm a base wallah it's even better than a leave 'cause I'll have each day pleasantly filled but every evening to myself and Sundays seems to be 'a day of rest' too.

A couple of months of this won't hurt me a bit – then I'll be ready to go on --- and on.

My new role
Also 30-12-44

So, the idea is that I'm here for two months to train new drivers. Knowing me as a jungle man as you do, you would not recognise me – coo, I'm choking myself with a collar and tie, wearing a normal battle dress, sitting in front of a blazing fire of pine cones – and that fire is in a real fire place.

I'm told that things start at 8 and finish at 6, the club and cinema are about a mile away! Tell me do: I thought I knew all about those civilian knives and forks and things but what does one do with the fifth knife from the right!?

How bad can they be?

I shudder to think what's going to happen now I'm going out with untrained drivers. On the way here I had several jangles myself and yesterday knocked off about 150 miles of flat going in 6 hours, but the vehicle's actual driver was a killer!

I can't recall every occasion but at least six times I had a quiet murmur to myself, "This is it Towny my lad" – but it never actually was. Hot sweat, cold sweat and all kinds in between were forced out of me – the only damage done to our wagon occurred when the boys failed to pull up as a gun, on tow, halted. The barrel of the gun turned the straight bars of the radiator grill into an attractive pattern, I turned the driver out of his seat and the bloke with the gun turned into a raving lunatic – who could blame him!

When I think of all the times, I gazed over the cliff edge and vehicles heading straight at each other for no apparent reason and then recall that he was supposed to be a trained driver. And now I'll be with untrained ones! I'll let you know even if I have to send the message written on a piece of cloud.

The new set up

I think I also mentioned my late orderly, the goon Hag Daal. Well, it was either him or me – he was already nuts so I packed him in cotton wool and set him loose in my platoon just as I was leaving.

Now I possess a bloke with a name that sounds like a sneeze who has some grey matter in the upper storey – trouble is that he's civilised. He's just asked me if I possess a teapot and a china cup – "Jeese bud' says I doanchuno there's a war on and an enamel mug serves every purpose imaginable."

"Ay, I know that but everyone here has a teapot so you should have one too" was the reply. I never knew just what problems domestic servants could provide – just imagine being landed with the whole bundle of waiter and the porter and the upstairs maid!

Glad it's only two months
6 -01-45

Your prayers have been answered – I've survived the first (and naturally the worst) week of living death sitting beside junglies whose one intent is to drive lorries off the road and over the cliff side.

I've already come to the conclusion that it's fortunate that my stay here will last only about two months. All the 'locals' are so well settled in that they are quite content to stay here for the rest of their lives.

Nice climate, no rationing and the war only affects those who discuss it in the club – bags of scandal, bags of parties and their picture in the Indian equivalent of The Tatler keeps everyone floating around in a sort of private heaven, untouched by the affairs of the world in general.

Very nice for a change but not my idea of the way that things should be until everyone can have a share.

Slash noticing the difference

Poor old Slash is noticing the difference as well – gone all 'civvy', wearing a collar for the first time in his life. Meeting thoroughbreds on the family hearth has rather unsettled him: if he growls in defiance or wags his tail at a prospective girl friend the result is the same – eyebrows shoot up and the frowns shoot down and people politely ask "What breed is he?"

We answer with our usual George Washington style "No breed at all simply a high –class pie- dog (Pariah!), don't you think he's sweet?"

One Week Later
13 -01-45

You'd think that because I'm in a new spot I should have tons to say on a variety of subjects. No, not this laddie – it seems to work the other way around. I'm around and about every day but usually only on a driving circuit whereas with the Coy I never knew whether I was on Gulliver's Travels or a Cook's Tour.

Driver training continues throughout January without undue incident. A trip to Cherrapunji (now called Sohra) – the wettest place on earth – was the only respite. With rainfall there of 39 inches in one day (enough for London for 18 months!) it was not a place to stay too long!

And then:

FEBRUARY '45

Put in charge – then summoned back to 64!
02-02-45

The other half of the D and M School goes under the name of David Kent – a nice guy. Last Sunday was his birthday celebration. On Monday he received a phone message telling him to pack his bag, hand over to me and clear off home to England on repat [*repatriation*].

Incidentally, he came out on the same convoy as me but isn't a low cheese member of the high-class Indian Army as I am.

Tuesday – Towny receives a signal 'You've had it chum, come back and do some work'. It seems that 64 have gone so far forward that they are scared I may forget that I belong to them, so in a day or two I too will have to pack my bags into my truck and go and see what the Jungle looks like again. Hence Tuesday night was an unhappy night and we have only one method of regaining happiness – celebration!

Another convoy to Cherrapunji filled Wednesday but as I was awful cold when I returned to the Colonial Hall I had to be filled with warm and soothing 'likker' to thaw out.

Medals!!

Yesterday I earned the OBE, George Cross, VC, ABC and YMCA. I tested the most durndest set of halfwits outside any looney bin you can think of. I was driven by 33 different people during the day and we only had one accident!

The thug who was clutching the wheel at the time continued to clutch it when he should have turned it and pranged into the cliff side at a rate of knots.

Towny, sitting by his side, took one glance at the high dive over the other edge of the road and decided not to grab the wheel, preferring a sudden halt of 20 feet on the level to the perils of a vertical drop of 200 feet!

After that we allowed ourselves time for lunch and then started again.

And more close shaves!

D'you know in the first hour after resuming I kind of saved my own life and that of the passengers four times by grabbing at handbrakes and doing a bit of remote-control steering – the last time one wheel was dangling over that confounded edge again! Needless to say, the nerves needed a little 'steadier' after such a day of ordeal.

So, my fren' I now feel as if it's the 'mornin' after the mornin' after the mornin' after etc'! Coo – what a war!!

Back to the Japs
3-02-45 and 13-02-45

I actually leave this luxurious life on Monday 5th to jangle forward to a place that the Japs have not yet left – if my next letter comes from Tokyo don't be surprised but keep writing to '64'. Nothing should surprise you now anyway!

I, following the approved tradition, postponed my leaving Day from the 5th to the 6th as the lad I was helping at the school was leaving for England on the 6th.

Last Monday night will be an outstanding item in the history of Towny the Younger as everyone came, everyone brought their own bottles and we had on loan a sergeant fellow who was a pre-war cocktail shaker in the Grand Hotel, Birmingham!

He shook – so did everyone else later!

Due to my murky past (I suppose) I survived better than most and sometime in the small hours delivered sagging bodies all over Shillong, all of whom persisted in struggling to semi – erect positions, gasping 'Heshajolly-goofella' and collapsing in tangled heaps all over the place.

Now for the great trek – 733 miles in 7 days. I left wearing battledress, over-coat, scarves, gloves and various other heat-giving devices. At the end of the last day a strip-tease act began which now leaves me wreathed in little but smiles. Each day odd items were discarded as we came south and if I go much further, I guess the locals are going to be rather embarrassed!

A day-by-day account of the trip could easily fill a book – but you are to be spared. I won't go into details – all I will say is that I'm passed the bumpy, dusty 'orrible area and am now once again in the places in the news.

It's very flat country, the roads are reasonably good and the weather the kind that one dreams about – you can take it that I'm rumbling along. I had a better look at the Chindwin as I came through it – it's a super sight which makes me wonder how the Thames was ever called a river and not a ditch. The next river is due to dwarf even this one.

The end of Slash

We had a minor disaster yesterday. Slash, my pup, after travelling to within 40 miles of here, was run over and killed when we stopped for a mid-day meal. It hurts like hell to not have him around 'cause he was an intelligent little hound and I'd had him for quite a time.

Apart from that everything went smoothly: I started with 3 lorries, 4 mo' bikes and 16 men and ended with 43 men and all those ducks and geese I'd been asked to bring – it looked just like a travelling circus with a large proportion of clowns (no wise cracks by request!).

Happily we arrived safely. Back to the fold!

PART 5

Mandalay, Rangoon and Victory

February – August 1945

Lt D.A. Townsend, Burma 1945.
Heading south to victory

CHAPTER 20

South to Mandalay

February – March 1945

An update on the Battle for Burma

This is an extract from E D Smith's Battle for Burma *– remember that Transport Company 64, which had now summoned Dad back, was part of the 19th Indian division:*

19 Division from 4 Corps set off on 4th December, crossing the Chindwin to the north of Sittaung. The plan was that if 19 Division found the going easy and the route suitable to its first objective at Pindebu, 7 Division would be ordered to follow the same course.

Having been knighted after Imphal, Lieutenant General Scoones had handed leadership of 4 Corps to Frank Messervy. Messervy's optimistic temperament made him the ideal choice for the open, fluid warfare that was to come, especially as 19 Division had a mercurial Welshman, Major – General Pete Rees, a veritable human dynamo who led from the front.

Soon Rees was to so inspire 19 Division that its exploits made the newspaper headlines in the United Kingdom – a remarkable feat at a time when 14 Army was still often referred to as 'The Forgotten Army'.

The emblem of 19 Division was a dagger; now the Dagger Division plunged its way forward with remarkable speed to capture Pindebu on 12th December. Rees's men captured highly revealing enemy documents which, augmented by reports from Burmese agents, showed that 15 Army (Japanese) was grouped round Mandalay like a clenched fist, with its main road and rail communications extending 60 miles to the south linking up with the important centre of Meiktila.

Slim was quick to appreciate that if Meiktila were seized by a sudden thrust, 15 Army would be deprived of vital supplies, separated from reinforcements and starved of its life-blood.

Strike Force for Meiktila

Thereafter little time was lost before launching a strike force for Meiktila. On 9ᵗʰ January 1945 19 Indian Division established a foothold when two small battalions crossed the Irrawaddy at Thabeilyun, a point some 60 miles north of Mandalay. Three days later another brigade from the same division landed a few miles south, using nothing more sophisticated than powered assault boats and raft – a remarkable feat of watermanship when it is remembered that the river is twice the width of the Rhine.

The Japs were convinced that 14 Army's main assault had begun and immediately sent their tried and tested 15 and 33 Divisions against Rees's bridgeheads, launching attack after attack in a desperate attempt to throw the Indian attack back into the river. But 19 Division stood firm.

It was to this front line action that Dad had now been summoned.

The letters now continue:

164 Coy RIASC Corp Tspt
(Troglodyte Terrace again)
Friday 16-02-45

Please note change of Co number and (2) that I'm underground again.

A lot has happened with a rush since I came home with the ducks – I'd hardly settled down when I was told to re-pack and join another company and here I am.

Apparently, my mate, the Colonel of the regiment, remembered inspecting Towny's platoon 'cause he posted me to a complete shower with the injunction to snap 'em out of it and turn 'em into soldiers!' That's what comes of being good and making impressions on Colonels. (Guess that's a natty piece of egotism but if I don't say I'm good no one else will – and what would you think!?)

So – having joined this bunch we immediately pack our kits again and move forward into the widest of wide-open spaces and here am I compelled to pencil in a hole in the ground.

This morning I went across yet another really big river[24] (1/2 mile wide) and it was like being out at sea, although it wasn't the waves that created the sick feeling! I guess "dere's Japs in dem dare hills" and we'll soon be moving forward again – coo!

---

24 That crossing was the Irrawaddy River.

Japs all around!

If either I or my mail becomes erratic, you'll know the reason why – the apple of Mrs Townsend's eye has got the pip and is pippin (or is it poppin) from pillar to post with his wagons, in and out of the little yellow baskets.

Anyway, I've made one gigantic discovery – unless someone slows me down, fairly soon I'll be able to send you a Chinese recipe for sarspa – I reckon that should make everyone – Towny included – blissfully happy.

Oh yes, a warning – beware of that game 'Monopoly'.

We played it the last night I was with 64 and normal 'ornery human (supposedly) beings turned into bloated capitalists and it was only by sheer will power that guns were kept off the table as our OC proceeded to swipe the kitty, only to be out swiped by a suburban subaltern – the language made me blush!

I'm just about to take out a convoy – not to anywhere with a name but just to another wide-open space which will look exactly like the one that I'm in now.

At Last – I can tell you where I am!
Weds 21-02-45

Now it can be told! The big bugs have relented and we can now say who we are, why we are, where we are and how we are!

Well, I guess I'm still ole Dauntless Don but 'why I am' can only be answered by Mrs T so we'll let that pass. Where I am is altogether different – d'you remember those balmy days, I spent in Shillong – So do I! Dear me, what super times they were – things are now slightly warmer in all respects.

I'm on the **No 1 Bridgehead at Singu with the 19th Indian Division** – a crowd which are making a name for themselves with a rush and being 'mentioned' in every bulletin at present. A nice crowd in fact who are definitely winning but, as I said, things are rather warm.

I've now made the crossing of the big river seven times, 1/2 a mile a time which if worked out very carefully will be seen to leave me on the China side – so it looks as tho' my wish to come home via China and America is still quite possible.

Being shelled!

Smarra fact, the only snag in the whole set up is Johnny Jap – he will persist in lobbing over the odd shell (not a fraction of those he receives) and odd shells aren't so good.

I'd just come home yesterday morning when 4 arrived – I was driving my jeep in front of a convoy – No 1 fell near enough to cover us with dust, No 2 blew the jeep and us down an old shell hole and the others were just noises in the distance – not very distant but I was looking for a hole to crawl in which was less uncomfortable than being under a jeep and so wasn't listening.

Trust Towny to think of comfort first!

And there is the story, no one hurt, jeep straightened up and driven away but one wheel had stopped a fragment and messed up the tyre tube, rim and everything.

Good old No 13 – lucky as ever!

So, how am I?

So, the answer to 'How I am' is – I'm fine. We've a lovely river, beautiful weather and enough soft sandy earth to dig to make it just like a holiday. (How I kid myself makes even me wonder!)

Talking of digging – the blisters are coming along just fine. My 'funk hotel' is certainly a safe place to be – but – somehow sleeping with innumerable mosquitoes in an 'ole with hot house temperature, where the dirt is falling through the roof all night and every time our guns go off the sides 'eave in, doesn't quite fit in with the festive spirit.

No sirree, the sooner we reach Mandalay the better – hoping that something is still standing!

Bombed in the bath!
27-02-45

I doubt if you've got any bad words in your vocabulary that I haven't in mine, but I've used up all my invective and am left weak and gasping, so if you could send me a few wicked words I'd be thankin' ye.

Those mothers, fathers, childless sons of the sun caught me napping the other eve — well, not exactly napping as Towny had decided after a quiet day, to take his bath and had only just stepped into the utility five inches of water and splashed himself from A–B when down whizzed the daily dozen.

I suppose my evasive action was as quick as anyone else's but diving into a dusty trench with nothing on and coming out covered in a film of mud doesn't help!

Go on now, laugh, I know you will but please don't overuse that fertile imagination – it was 'orrible!

MARCH '45

Japs heading south
1-03-45

I'll first give you the set up as it is at present.

We're still winning, and the Japs seem to have continued their hike southwards from this locality: we can no longer hear the small arms fire and even Pooping Pete and Seven-thirty Sarah, their two big guns, no longer disturb my equilibrium (haven't used that word for ages!).

No, all we have now is the Singu Serenade – lots and lots of gunner types who never seem to sleep and whose sole intent is to keep everybody else awake – especially the yellow whatsits at the receiving end.

The only clouds in view are ones of dust, palm trees swaying.

Picture this: me sitting on a pile of tyres with my back against a palm tree – ordinary tyres but not an ordinary palm tree. Its 3-foot thick at the bottom, charred and burnt on one side with bits knocked out by bombs and such like.

It shoots up for about 60 feet and stops – not a leaf or anything – the top has been blown off making it look like a factory chimney. It stands in what was once a house. The garden is a jungle, the house a dozen cindered poles stuck in the ground.

My wagons are dispersed all over the place but the junglies persist in running over the piles of ash of buildings that were – and picking up nails by the dozen in their tyres. Hence me sitting on a few waiting to be repaired.

The garden jungle is full of 'holes in the ground' – home!

My platoon office, a plank, balanced on two oil drums, with two piles of papers held down by stones super-imposed on the plank, occupies a strategic position where any mid-night marauder would trip over it. I know they would – I've already done it myself!

Planes, Parachutes and Pagodas

Apart from the bees and things the air is also crammed with Dakotas and parachutes – our grub, mail and everything arriving that way – we are glad to see 'em.

Whichever way I look (provided the vista isn't blotted out by the trees) I can see a pagoda. The place swarms with them because in the good old days Burmese villages were graded in the snobbish social register by the number of pagodas erected.

This place must have been snob-de-luxe but now they are in varying stages of decay – we heard a vague rumour that Berlin had suffered in the same way.

That last letter was written on 1st March. The next one is written on the 13th. The events of the days in between had been intense. Quoting from E D Smith's Battle for Burma *once again:*

Rees, at the head of 19 Division had been pushing forward towards Mandalay and by the first week of March his troops were within gunshot range of Mandalay Hill. Thereafter for several days, a bitter struggle was waged for the monastery on top of the hill overlooking the town.

This was a battle that really did make all the front pages and is still talked about today.

First 'Service Corps Wallahs' into Mandalay!
13 -03-45

Jeese, things have been so hectic, the days so long and so full, sleep so rare, that it'll take some time for me to recall all that has happened.

It must be about a fortnight ago that the world went kinda mad as far as I and my pal were concerned. We had to take every wagon we could lay our hands upon, dash away and collect a load of infantry and there we were.

A day or two later we found ourselves part of a mobile column whose task was to reach Mandalay – and we did!

We went straight across country, not a road of any kind – over paddy fields fording rivers, all sorts. In the end the tanks and infantry got out and walked (you know what I mean!) and went and had a bash at the Japs.

Towny jangled along the administrative wagons, cigs, food, ammo etc and didn't meet a guide 'till he was ½ mile from the big city.

The guide said that we should be miles back, which didn't help much, so I share the privilege with my pal to be the first Service Corps wallahs to arrive

The reception committee didn't exactly hang the flags out and I've a good selection of blisters again from trench digging.

My oppo wounded

Now, I'm back on the old convoy job again – to and from the big city on a daily service and it doesn't leave much time, especially as I now own all the wagons since my pal got wounded.

Do you know, just at present my war aims have reverted to a post-war thistlebed and a reservoir full of ice-cold beer – more so since I saw the local brewery go up in flames – but keep the old steak and chips simmering, there's a pal.

St Patrick's Day
17-03-45

If it isn't old St Patrick's Day itself – I've taken it as a holiday! S'like this see – Young Towny, having spent six days as the point of a spearhead and another six running the Singu-Mandalay Express – dusty convoys which make me wonder why I ever was interested in motorcycle trials – became rather browned off and if I may say so – a trifle insubordinate!

My pal who owns the other platoon had been wounded in the first jaunt, leaving me with all the wagons. And so, I complained!

An OC and 2i/c from way back in HQ, surrounded by bumph, sitting back as armchair critics, kinda riled me, so I said "Ooh, I'm sorry, it's you I'm writing to!"

Anyway, the 2i/c has taken today's convoy and I've stuck around and helped our workshop guy (an Irishman begorra), to help him celebrate his national saint.

I beg to state that I'm now back on form.

And what a day – MAIL! Really, they are the goods, the bees knees, the answer to everything – well you know how it is. If every guy had someone behind him to push out the laughs and the griff as you do, the war would be over tomorrow (well maybe the day after!).

And your right as usual –I guess I wouldn't have missed the last few years of travel –better than sticking around in an office! No sirree – what to do next is the only thing that puzzles me!

And don't worry – your letters will always find me. The fact that you send a letter to 'A' when I'm at 'B' matters not. Towny's Trucks Un-limited dash around so much that we are here, there and everywhere all at once. That said, I can't dash around much more as I'm told there is a Jap MP on the next cross-roads and I'm not on speaking terms with him as we haven't been introduced!

Sssh – I've been making eyes at a Burmese matron who owns the field in which I'm living – and I've doctored her husband's arm – she's coming across with a chicken – tonight we eat!!

Back from another run – six days later
23-03-45

Wow!! I'd just come in from a long and dusty convoy; been bumped and bounced and battered, like a coffee bean in the grinding process (not too technical I trust), had missed breakfast and at 3pm was dreaming of a late lunch, pre- war iced orangeades and a reclining divan surrounded by dusty (whoops! dusky) slaves with whopping great fans of peacock fevers: was mopping the weary brow from which fountains of persp were gushing- and at the same time, with the spare hand, trying to tug off an irksome boot – when sudden like the 2 i/c rolled up and said 'Here's your lovely mail' – or something like it. And to be sure – there it was!

Of course, you started on the wrong note by asking me if I felt good but there, I looked around and found that here also the sun was shining and the sky so blue and life began to brighten no end.

Ferrying released prisoners

When our boys climbed the local fort, they found a lot of civvy internees all waiting to be freed – and Towny's Trucks Incorp bailed them out to their new abode.

The folks have had a really tough time during the past 3 years – ill-treated by the Japs and often bombed, shelled and machine gunned by us during the advance (all unnecessary like and no harm meant of course).

Now they are sitting back with glazed eyes, lapping up decent food, newspapers and falling on tooth-brushes and tooth-paste with rapture – and I'm helping 'em do it in between times.

Ay, you've hit the mark again – our grub is pretty good all round these days and the odd egg and occasional chick eases the situation no end. Even so it looks like I'll be leaving 19 for pastures new – and who knows, there may be a boat waiting at Rangoon.

CHAPTER 21

Rangoon, Victory and Saving the General

April – June 1945

Transfer to 2 British Division

I'm adding a bit of editorial input here just to keep the flow of the story. Whilst 19 Division had played a very significant role in taking Mandalay a major battle had been waging further south at Meiktila which was a key part of the Japanese supply line. The Allies won the battle after extremely heavy fighting and the next goal was to head south to free Rangoon before the monsoons started.

The need for major convoys, troop and armament movements were therefore not in Mandalay with 19 Indian Division but in moving further south – the role of 2 British Division, part of 33 Corp under General Stopford.

Dad was transferred, complete with the rest of his transport company – number 164 – to 2 British Division just after he wrote that last letter on 23rd March '45.

Letters continue:

A Very Busy Six Days!
28-03-45

Address: Budda's Bathroom, Popeye's Pagoda

My but it's been busy. Let's get the story in the right order and you'll see what I mean.

My jeep creaked into the Company lines at 4 pm, moaning and groaning in every spring saying "Lookee here mate, we've been out for six days, what about a spot of grease?" I was moaning and groaning back 'cause I haven't got any springs or shock absorbers and could have done with them – often.

For once I was not too happy – 500 of our kind of miles in 6 days, sleeping anywhere and everywhere and lots of the dust I've mentioned doesn't make for song and laughter – besides its hot these days and the ice cream parlour isn't functioning yet.

You see what I mean – I was cheesed. Well, things kinda looked up after that.

I 'er, I 'er, well I stripped and my orderly threw half a dozen 4-gallon cans of water over me (talk about the bare facts!) and then I dipped into the utility 5 inches and removed the other 3 layers of grime. Then a change of clothes, a cup of char, a pull at the mobile furnace (my last fill of tobacco too) and said 'bring in the mail' just like that – using the voice that stops clocks and makes full grown men tremble, like the maids of old did before dem guys in armour started the chivalry racket.

Having mail made things so much better!

To give you an insight to those hectic 6 days:

– first convoy to Maymyo [*40 miles west of Mandalay*], six more trips across the river (still leaves me on the wrong side), dead Japs everywhere and live Japs too close for my liking.

– I discovered that Mandalay should be spoken of in the past tense – as there is hardly a building standing – and to finish, a nice spot of line-shooting when I met the Colonel – I took out my two grenades saying, "I guess I won't need these in this back area." Happily, he saw the joke.

While I'm out on trips the Company shoots all over the map on its own account and my homing instincts have to be trained to pigeon pitch. When I found them today, I found that we'd taken over a bombed-up village and I'd been settled into a pagoda to sleep right at the feet of the Buddha. So, I tapped the old forehead on the doorstep just to show the gods that I was on their side and didn't wish to embarrass old Bud when I hit the hay.

APRIL '45

By the time the next letter is written a week later on 3ʳᵈ April, Dad is in a field hospital. With such a hectic period just completed it is probable that sheer exhaustion was at least part of the cause. As ever however he manages to make a joke of it!

In field hospital!
3-04-45
I'll give you free hundred and firty free guesses where I am just now – and you'd still be wrong.

Yes, I'm still way down south but ---- I'm a temporary resident in a 'field ambulance'.

At some time on the recent travels one of my junglies must have swung me some dud water and here am I, most happy in my service, with a tummy full of dysentery. It's wonderful!!!

Behind my bed is a little chart with 'BED REST' written on it in whopping great letters. In rather smaller letters it says 'fluids – pills' and even smaller gives a temperature and a pulse rate which both remind me of the Brooklands lap record or a snooker break by Walter Lindrum.

Still, there it is and here am I – no convoys and dashing around for at least a fortnight (I hope!), bags of liquid refreshment and no grub for a day or two – and bed – and rest; another lad has just come in and he seems to have a wireless set – yippee!!

Actually I arrived in on the 1st, straight in from a convoy – one of my usual bullock cart-track and paddy-field affairs, so I kinda spent yesterday in coming round to normal – or is my normal state abnormal? I wouldn't know.

Anyway, I'm round to it now and in a day or two, when I've pushed out letters to some of the most deserving cases, I'll concentrate on the final episode of the travels – Abbottabad – Imphal in one mighty swoop.

And true to his word he did write that final episode all 34 pages of it.

A Japanese pyre and more besides

I must tell you one thing that happened before I came in here. Have you ever had a passion to have a ruddy big bonfire, a real super-duper blaze up? Well, I have to admit that I've always had a yen to have one of my own – and I've had it – all by mistake!

Just after last writing to you I rolled up my convoy into a burnt-up village for the night and proceeded to make myself at home. It didn't take too long to find out that a few Japs had outstayed their welcome – four of 'em, very high and not so almighty, so we decided to cremate them on the spot.

Piles of wood and lashings of petrol for the boyos, a little safety trail of high octane and a piece of burning rag for us and whoosh – up went the whole caboodle – but so did the two houses next door!

Ooo, I was surprised – until I learned that one of my bright specimens had walked nonchalantly away, pouring petrol with the can upside down and so laid a trail around the huts.

I felt like pinning the thugs ears a yard apart – I could have as there is nothing in the middle to stop it – but the army always has a rule or regulation for every occasion, so I sat back and enjoyed the blaze!

Out already!
8-04-45
Though his letter of 3rd April had said he was to be in hospital 'for at least a fortnight'
he was out ahead of schedule after just 8 days – somehow true to character!

Yah, your too late with your sympathy – I'm out of dock and am ticking along like a time bomb running on Double Summertime – right back on form and nicely rested thank you.

I think Doctors are too, too divine – mine feeding me on cement pills for the first 3 days – (156 of them!) and chicken and beer for the remainder of the stay – can you wonder at me wanting to take the week-end excursion to Rangoon!

500 miles since the last letter
14-04-45
Phew – since I last wrote a week ago, I've been tearing around like a Walt Disney Goofy and now, by using every available finger, have decided that it must be about Sunday 15th [*it was actually the 14th!*]

You know, the more I see of Burma – and I've seen about 500 miles of it in this last little effort this week, the more I wonder just how pleased Johnny Jap must be to get out of it. I think when folks at home start imagining what Burma is like, the first thing they think of is dense, impenetrable jungle, full of animals, things that creep and crawl, thickly populated with bush-hatted squaddies, who slink around on their stomachs – and after such an effort of the mind they're rather vague as to the rest.

What Burma is really like?
Me, being big-hearted, I'll give you the complete and down-to-earth reality of what it's really like. Here goes:

The way we came:
Coming the way we came, the first couple of hundred miles conforms to popular opinion – jungle.

But – it is much more like Epping Forest than anything produced by MGM in the jungle line:

- the trees are fairly widely spaced, there seem to be no animals apart from the occasional jackal – all the rest have been scared away from the war area – and, as we came through in the dry season, the creepy crawlies were present only in their thousands instead of millions.

- During the monsoon they all come to life and things aren't so good. And our bush-hatted heroes – and even the Japs- never wander too far from the tracks, as it is too easy to lose oneself in the trees.
- As far south as Mandalay the country is like a billiard table – flat, like the fen country, cultivated with rice, tomatoes, palms, and banana plantations; dusty, un-interesting.
- After that, travelling southwards as far as I've been, its simply bloody awful! Miles and miles of the most useless country imaginable – undulating, rocky and sandy, covered in prickly shrubs, blazing sun and no shade. The only trees are scattered clumps of frowsty palms which only seem to increase the barrenness of the area. Water is rare!!

Don't get me wrong – I'm not ticking, just passing the griff, 'cause I'm sitting as pretty as I could wish for.

I'm on detachment from the Company (which will mean a delay in receiving mail from your end, so don't worry if I don't answer too rapidly) and having now crossed the river <u>20</u> times I'm parked under a huge cluster of trees just half a mile from its bank. Its lovely!!

A simple job, no-one to push me around, sufficient time to look under the bonnets of my wagons, two bottles of wallop – and the river – coo, who could want for more!

Monsoons Arrived Early
22-04-45

Local news from here: (1) yesterday the stars forgot to tell that it would rain (2) that I'd be out in it (3) that tracks across paddy fields would revert to their original mud.

I've a sneaking feeling that the weather isn't running true to form – I mean the monsoon has made much better time than ever before – we recover the bogged jeep tomorrow!

A period of 'local duties' follows with little detail being given of them in the letters of 22nd and 29th April. Then back to action by the letter of the 5th May '45.

MAY '45

Getting Cracking Again
5-05-45

I'm due to get cracking again. Three weeks of 'local duties' have finished, my wagons look like Olympic show models, we're about 150 miles behind the Japs and we have to catch them up so's we don't go 'stale' – and in my case, I was getting 'browned' off being anchored in one spot.

Tomorrow we're due to do 100 miles, the same the next day and after that a 6-day non-stop trip which should put the jeep mileage back to form. Better yet, I'm told the next bit of Burma is an improvement on anything we've seen yet – which should help a lot!

Same letter – Sunday 6th May

Passing through areas of destruction

We've done todays' spot of mileage and it's been no better than anything seen previously – except we've passed through the oil field areas and believe me, our lads in '42 did a good job of its destruction.

The Japs have made no attempt to touch the mess and the whole area adds up to the biggest scrap heap I've ever seen.

I'm doing all this a bit hasty like as, when I've whipped it orf I've to arrange for this 6-day affair and it's a bit of a do.

Food, 'gas' and even water has to be accounted for somehow – so do my hordes of thugs, so do 90 wagons – and they can't all be guaranteed not to break down – I even have to organise myself and decide what to take for six days in comfort in a jeep – and it's bound to rain! Cor – and he likes the life!

So, while the war in Burma was still progressing and the Japs were yet to succumb, things in Europe were very different. Think for a moment about the dates and you will realise that victory in Europe, 'VE Day' – 8th May '45 – was just two days away.

The troops in Burma had radio, newspapers and also had a regular newspaper of their own – The SEAC Times.

They knew what was going on – as Dad showed in his next letter:

Congratulations on VE Day!
12-08-45

Be ye sober lass? I mean to say hast recovered from the wayward wanderings of victory? The whole thing hasn't really sunk into us out here yet – they've put it into words of two syllables so's even I could understand it:

'The War in Europe is Over!'.

Nice work – send a few guys out here now to complete the job.

Rangoon fallen

You were wrong – Rangoon fell without my aid, I think I menched the fact that I was back doing a base-wallah job and making the engines tick again.

Still, we are now at the back of the front – can't say where but there's a sign which says (when in xxxxx do what the Proman's do[25]) and there's a hell of a lot of Japs between me and Rangoon on this 'ere road – and they don't like the heat any more than we do.

First 'flick' for 3 months

Just to prove that the last week has been one that will go down in history, I must include the indisputable fact that I've seen a flick after a three-month break. A good one too *The Way Ahead* with David Niven and all the boys. – and Mickey Mouse – what more could we want!

Yes – I found an immobile, mobile cinema and cut in on the deal. In fact, I've hopes that it'll be around when I return from the next convoy – open air and all that – but hot!

Cor, I'm volunteering for the next trip to Hades, to cool off! It's been scorching recently and if the wagons aren't moving, we don't touch 'em between 11 am – 4 pm, although we could easily fry eggs on them – if we had eggs!

Now I've to dash along and catch up on my trucks – they left half an hour ago and will give the Japs a lift if I don't stop 'em!

Heading south to Rangoon
20-05-45 [8 days later]

Time to whip off a quick 'un again; Picture Towny in an ever de-creasing circle, leading one convoy and trying to act as rear guard to the one in front.

---

25 Prome was the location – 180 miles to the north of Rangoon.

Wondering if he has enough petrol to reach the next stage, wondering if those storm clouds will open up a torrent.

Tomorrow I'm off on a 9-day jaunt to Rangoon. This trip should be whizzo and it looks as though we will have to take a long route pushing up a mileage of about a thousand before I return to my roost.

Towny's Tours Incorp are extending their scope to big stuff at last – any time you're out this way just raise a thumb and we'll give you a lift anywhere; Burma Bus Coy would be a more appropriate name for us at present.

I had a letter from home today which confirmed my worst fears – there was plenty of booze available on VE Day and lots of people made the most of it – drunken types that they are – and I missed it!

Cor. A pint with a frothy top – just to cool the perspiring brow. I doubt it would touch the sides!

Is anybody interested in us?

The ban has been lifted on our past wanderings – we can say where we've been and who we've been with, but hell, whose interested in history. The school kids in the 20th C. will curse all the present-day newsmakers in maybe even more striking terms than I commented on Magna Carta and all the other ruddy dates one had to remember!

Wow!! The big noise whose crowd are using my wagons has started the front ones off – I'll have to pack in quickly and fall in at the rear. Sorry for the hell of a rush but things happen like this at times – I'll drop this in at my HQ as I whizz by.

Back from Rangoon
29-05-45 (9 days later)

I'm 'home' again once more, only whilst I was away my home moved by about 100 miles – we never know where we are going to end up or why!

Seven days on the road and a days' sight seeing in the big city produced only 836 miles. I say 'only' as I was expecting more but the company came out to meet us.

Seven days on a B**** B*** road [*just so that you know the asterisk's are actually in the letters – I am not taking out the expletives!*] which has left me feeling like an underdone jelly – one calls it a road as its marked on the map as such – the other things we call it are much more accurate and I leave you to imagine the adjectives that we use.

Even so it was an interesting trip and I've now seen real ships for the first time in 3 years – and seen sailors too.

Lots of streets in China town are out of bounds because a number of Japs haven't had the time or sense to clear out and are still tucked away in the area. One thing about returning to civilisation is that you get news and I beg to admit that I was shook.

We had travelled down a road on one side of the country, were due to return by another route 100 odd miles to the west: the news we had was that there were 12,000 Japs in between the roads and about 40,000 Japs scattered on the Japan side of the road we'd just travelled: ooooo-er!!

I still think I saw half a dozen dressed in coolie clothes but couldn't very well stop my hundred wagons to make enquiries: nevertheless, it is true that when we arrived home at 4 pm the road was open; at mid-night it was blocked and a few more Nips were streaking eastwards.

And they say the war in Burma is over!

Today I'm ticking over as far as the situation permits, although there is a ton of army returns to be pushed out at the end of the month – tomorrow I'm off again – a series of 3-day trips.

Things are really much more pleasant now though, as we've left that barren area which was so hot and useless. Nowadays we knock around in jungle country and further south, a high patch of rice country which is flatter than any pancake for hundreds of miles – a push-bikers paradise!

JUNE '45

It's finally getting too much
5-06-45

I'm in a moody mood. I'm kinda tongue tied before I start which I must admit is strange for Towny.

- Maybe it's the hot-house weather, I'm the stickiest and clammiest I've been for a long, long time.
- maybe it's my corns, I've just finished 1200 miles in the old jeep and am feeling rather tender in the rear.
- maybe it's just because the travelling has been, to me, so very normal that it doesn't warrant special mention! Except perhaps, the slight episode of a river crossing – no bridge and a swift current – jeeps had to be towed across and of course mine went down a hole.

Coo, I, watching it from the bank, made animal noises as the part that ticks went under the muddy water, to leave only the windscreen and the driver's chocolate torso showing – and blithely crossed on the next wagon to repair the damage.

However, by the time we were winched across, having been bogged in the middle for half an hour the works had dried out and were running! Even that is enough to drive a normal guy speechless but we all agree that I'm somewhere west of sub-normal so that can't be the reason can it.

It's the bugs!

If I was asked to make conversation with anyone right now, I think I'd make the topic 'bugs'. What I'd say about them would largely depend on the other client. I mean there are so many ways of saying how bloody awful things are aren't there – and Aunt Agnes might frown if she heard me genning up a sailor on creeping horribles!!

The fact remains that the flying and crawling things just about fill all 24 hours of the day – so many penetrate the mosquito net by devious means that even the hours of slumber are not trouble free – all due, no doubt to the damp and warm atmosphere – a Kew Hot House with the lid off.

Mossy's and the usual hordes of flies are the lesser worries – of the airborne invasion the pin head size mango-flies, which whizz around like dots in front of your eyes and the beetle bombers – armour plated and by the noise they make, radial engined big 'uns, drive one bats.

Then we have a delectable variety of ants, caterpillars, centipedes, scorpions spiders, slugs, snails and snakes and other things too – that have no names in polite society – which whizz, buzz, bite, sting and get in the jam and live for one thing only – to fall headlong into ones newly filled glass and then splash and splutter 'til you either whip 'em out or drink 'em!

I could go on and on but the thought of you sitting back there itching and wriggling 'cause I'm describing the local beautie, is enough to stop me. I'll stop

An unusual 2-week gap in letters occurs here – by the time they resume it's time for the Victory Parade in Rangoon!

Words with the Colonel
23-06-45

Either the whole world has gone mad or I have – maybe the answer is obvious I find, by referring to the book of rules, that I last wrote on the 5th and now look at the ruddy date. All the words I can think of to describe recent happenings would make you blush and so all I'm left to do is say 'Thank Christ its over!'

Did I, in the last effort, tell you that I was about to go to Rangoon again? Well, I went any way and took a party down to the Victory Parade and everything was very sweet apart from the mud and the rain – Lord High Cheese Louis was soaked to the skin – same as me!

I left 164 on the 9th, three days to the big city, 2 days back, all the clothing we possessed soaking and no means of drying it, no cigarettes for the lads – we thought we'd earned a rest.

Oh no, the Promans have funny ideas about things and we had to go back again – my jeep registered 1178 miles from the time I left home 'til the time I returned, my boys were going to sleep over their wheels, and we'd had it – and yet someone wanted us to do yet another trip.

That's when the Colonel and I had words – no promotion of course but no convoy either and time to have a decent sleep and write some letters. It was worth it!

TOWNY SAVES THE GENERAL
24-06-45

I came, I swore, I conked out – that was yesterday. Now I've found a ration, had a nice nights sleep, told my platoon to go away to, er – well they've gone, and I can continue where I left off.

Now, I know your itching to hear about Towny and the General – here's the unexpurgated griff in a plain wrapper.

The victory parade was over (and I'll tell you more about that too later) and I was motoring quietly round in the 15 minutes of dusk, looking for any unit where I knew a guy would feed me for the night.

My headlights fell on another jeep, bonnet up, bodies peering into the part that ticks: I caught a glimpse of a red hat and said to myself: "Towny this is where you do yourself a bit of good, it may be the Colonel" (that was before I had my fourth row with him of course!)

So, I apply the anchors and using my best Harrow voice ('arrow 'igh street) murmured "Can I be of any assistance SIR?"

Caw, up springs the body and it's a real live Major General – I sorta gulp buts its ok – he's gulping much more than I am.

"Oh, er, yes, er thank God you're here; yes, please help me, er, what's the time; seven? Ooo, er, I'M DINING WITH THE SUPREMO AT 7.30, what shall I do?" [*'Supremo' is Lord Louis himself!*]

There was only one thing for it – I gave him a direct order, 'GET IN!' – and then asked him where he wanted to go.

Too bad, he was lost – which made two of us, so I asked him if he was on the parade that morning – I guess I collected a fishy stare, but the answer was affirmative, and I gathered he could find his way home from there.

We motored!

It was the only road I knew and after receiving the gentle hint "please don't trouble to go slow for me" we flew down to his HQ – time 7.10.

'Come up for a drink while I change'.

Well, Gen or no Gen, I never refuse an offer like that, so up we toddle, where Towny is rather shaken to find a Colonel and a Lt Colonel dashing round in ever de-creasing circles trying to act as batmen.

Very interesting too – especially when "Give this chap a drink, he's helped me" resulted in both of them diving for the same bottle.

Still, three drinks were poured (nice gin too!) and the Lt Col is busy peering up at my shoulders to see what has crawled out of the cheese; being a small man he asks me to sit down and "make myself at home."

He sees the awful truth, so I take a large swig at my noggin in case he asks for it back – at which point there's a cry from the General without "no time for a bath, pour me a drink too."

I finish my drink, accept a cigarette, instinctively smell it to see if its musty and then realise it's a <u>real</u> English one.

In dashes the Gen, picks up one of the remaining drinks on the table, knocks it back (very well-trained elbow action) says "Is this mine?"' to everyone and "let's go" to me.

The Colonel who has been sitting quiet looks horrified – and then to me – the light dawns – it was his drink which disappeared down the hatch!

We go and I deliver the old boy spot on time, although he still has a dewy brow. Later I go back to his HQ to enquire about his jeep; it had arrived back and the Lt Colonel (also damp on top), went rash and said 'come up for another one '.

Phew, I was so rash I said "Yes" and then asked him who I had been helping:

"GENERAL RANCE, new out from home to look after the Burma Civil Affair." Very interesting but it meant nothing to me and that was that. I meet 'em!

Major General **Sir Hubert Elvin Rance** *GCMG GBE CB had just been appointed 'Director of Civil Affairs' in Burma.*

A year later, In August '46 he replaced Reginald Dorman-Smith as Governor of British Burma and held that office, being the last to do so, until 4ᵗʰ Jan '48 when Shwe Thaik, president of Burma, took office.

My but that was a chance meeting!

The victory parade

Now the parade itself was pretty good – everyone was there – and the poor yank contingent had full packs. Three bands, Chinese, Navy, RAF, Ghurkhas, Burma Army (!), and tons of Indians and a couple of battalions of PBI [*Poor Bloody Infantry*] produced the goods.

Lord Louis gave them the once over, mounted his dais and the heavens broke as he began to say his piece. Boy that rain went through everything – and then I took my trucks to the end of the procession route to collect the damp corpses. S'lovely life!!!

CHAPTER 22

Someone Tell our Japs its Over!

July – August 1945

War torn areas revisited.
27-06-45
Strike-alight I'm off again and can't do a thing about it. Off for another 6 days. Before I go let me tell you a little bit about our visit to Prome. The Japs in '42 apparently were their usual nasty selves, and they had some bombers, and we did not. – Prome took it.

It was knocked inside out about, two buildings left intact and they have since suffered from shells; anyway, the residents cleared out to the jungle and the jungle took over the town – weeds, creepers and undergrowth are now everywhere.

Mere foundations and fireplaces can't be seen in the tangle of vegetation, the remaining walls and bits of pagodas are camouflaged into the most fantastic, shaped trees you ever saw; just what I imagined the lost city of the Incas would look like.

My own present 'home' first appeared as a weed patch surrounded by three creeper covered walls, surmounted by a rose bower (less roses!).

We cut and dug and cleaned up a foot of earth and a few scattered tiles and discovered beneath, a good concrete floor; we found gaps in the walls where windows had been, the ramblers gave way to a wooden framework of a roof. That is now covered with tarpaulins and 'home' is almost comfortable.

I cut my way through the 'garden', discovered a hidden wall and fell down a trench – full of Jap ammo which I should imagine caused more than one Jap quarter-bloke to commit hari – kari.

Prome is the answer to the bug-hunters' prayer – the mosquitoes have been starved for three years and are making up for lost time!

JULY '45

Three subalterns running the company
8-07-45

I've left the Inca city for more Eastern climes as the Japs thought the war was over since I'd been missing for a time.

It's been a right busy time, all three of us subaltern stooges now running a company which at present stretches over 350 miles! The OC is on a boat due for release; the 2i/c left to command another coy and 164 marches on – and on – and on!

Moving Burmese families

But we're doing fine, at least at up to 4 pm today, which time I managed to evict the last of a Burmese family from its residence and dress the bottles by the right on the heirloom sideboard.

It's a nasty job moving folks out of their homes – especially when it's raining like this (thanks for re-assuring me that the sun has not disappeared from the universe), but it has to be done and it looks as if I'm again to sleep in the same place for several nights in succession. Yippee!!

Convoys explained
15-07-45

Today I'm cheating, refusing to do a stroke from lunchtime onwards. I'm going to retire to my couch, remove the 10lb mud caked boots and sink into a sonorous slumber. Coo, I'm going drowsy in anticipation.

Subjects are scarce at present owing to an overdose of the devil's creation – WORK. And it's all in large doses. Let me put it this way so's you get yourself aligned with the situation:

From your holiday place in Cambridge take 120 lorries, driven by semi-madmen to NE London (about the same size as Rangoon). One of your 150 men can read, write and speak English but can't read a road map. Of the rest, two thirds speak French of which you've a smattering, the remainder speak Chinese. [*This was a big change from 19 Indian Division where most of the drivers were Indians and spoke Urdu – which Dad had learned as part of his training. I do not know the detail but evidently a lot of Chinese and French speaking drivers were in 2 British Division.*]

Some of your wagons have to go to load at Stepney, others at Ilford, Enfield and Barking – you've to collect them together at Woodford and return to

Cambridge tomorrow morning and have to feed the thugs at all normal meal times!

Aye, it puzzles me at times too – and out here most of the trucks refuse to tick like a Swiss made watch and make noises comparable with 'The Rockets' forebears.

Oh yes – you do the trip twice a week and try to run (ruin?) the lives of your company on the 'at home' days. Can you wonder that we go chasing butterflies, stripped to the waist and have evolved a special clog dance for rum issue nights!

JAPS still getting in the way
23-07-45 (8 days later)
Why? Why me? I'm not due for release or anything so no-one should be trying to get the last ounce out of me. Then why?

10,000 ruddy Japs want to go home – across our road and have started to do so – blocking the road in the process. Then up comes a back room boy with a letter addressed to me saying: "You will proceed to xxxxx with ammo at once" – the place being the other side of the japs.

Coo – 'will ', 'at once'. I guess I prefer the days of chivalry – this modern idea of 'you've had it, get cracking' almost leaves me cold – it would if I didn't sweat so much.

They don't even give you time to say "I already have sufficient lines to shoot in an English Pub – how about some other lad having a 'do'?"

No – they give me two armoured cars and some good advice – 'go like hell'. We went and we've come back – you don't know just how relieved I am to be home once more. My, my – where's that boat!

Time and time again in the letters, I get the impression that Dad is not telling the whole story – glossing over the dodgy bits. The above tale is perhaps as near as he gets to saying 'I was really scared!' Who wouldn't be?!

AUGUST '45

Peace on its way?
5-08-45
Peacetime again! Well, almost – I mean to say, there are no Japs left hereabouts and a couple of days ago I went to a place and was told "come back tomorrow", leaving me to twiddle my thumbs.

A day off!! True, it was in the middle of no-where but I crept back into my truck 'caravan' and made up my mind to become mentally blank for an hour or two!

And 'peace' was coming. The day after this letter was written, 6ᵗʰ August 1945, the Atom Bomb was dropped on Hiroshima. A second Atom Bomb was dropped on Nagasaki on 9ᵗʰ August. These would result in the surrender of Japan.

Someone tell our Japs its over!
12-08-45

Drunk again I suppose, I hope – I mean it is over isn't it? The news kinda percolates through but no one has fully realised the fact as it seems all of a 'sudden like' – and now we are faced with an awful problem – who's going to tell our Japs??

These silly little men know nothing – not even that Japan has been bombed; believe nothing you tell 'em and stick at nothing, what to do?

Same letter continues on 19-08-45.

Oh! Oh!! The injustice of it all! I know just what you're thinking but you are wrong – abso- bally-lutely wrong. I haven't disappeared under the table for a week, beery smile and clutching bottle to breast. Honest!

True enough, I did my share of celebration – but there was I in the middle of no-where, alone with five bottles of real English wallop – Whitbread's: and I've earned another medal 'cause I made it last for 3 days – I celebrated anyway.

But someone's been dropping atomic bombs around here or something – since I last started this ignoble effort I've been whizzing up and down Burma like a bloody blue-bottle or words to that effect – cor, I'm not sure if I'm going, coming, or gone with the wind.

S'like this – I'm doing my stuff 'a whizzing' when up rolls a guy with a beautifully sealed letter – it was really a shame to open it, but I hardened the old heart and cracked open the wax – and nearly passed out on the spot!

Item 1: the rest of the company will arrive tomorrow, prepare site, fix guides, arrange food, accommodation, petrol, water and what have you.

Item 2: take over 31 vehicles from another coy and put them on duty right away (as if I have 31 drivers in my pocket).

The boys whipped up a cup of char to bring me round and then up rolls my Indian 2i/c with "Sahib much trouble what to do?"

Three so and so's had deserted, or at least forgotten to come home at night, another had lost his pay book, two managed to ram other vehicles and 2000 cigarettes had disappeared from a loaded truck.

Say, didn't I give you a list like this last time? I guess I have to make a rugby 15 out of my babies instead of a football 11!

Enough – let me tap my nut on the ground and say "Salaam, I'm glad to know you in peacetime!"

Peacetime – huh!
23-08-45

The RAF have celebrated by not sending a plane here for over a week, resulting in no mail going or coming out and I wouldn't want you to think that I'm still in the nasty mood I was in a few days back.

No, no, indeed, I'm on the up and up. I've fixed all of my delinquents and given them ample time to squat behind barbed wire and reflect on the bitterness of life and even more time to work out a solution to mend their ways – in between, their soliloquies, the odd spot of pack drill and pick and shovel work, helps clear the mind and keep the fat down. Hard hearted Horatio – that's me.

Better still, I'm trying to fix a short leave in Calcutta so's I can accumulate a few civvies for the boat – and after. Green drill suitings, battledress pattern, slung revolver and bush hat will be hardly the attire to attend civic functions, burial and garden parties in too, too cold England!

Now I must tear myself away and prepare for another Lt Col who wants to inspect my platoon and gaze soulfully at the latrines. Peacetime – huh!

SEPTEMBER '45

Time to celebrate!!
4-09-45

To satisfy your curiosity – we did see off quite a number of bottles at the time but as a marrer o' fact last night was <u>the</u> night as far as we were concerned.

It took me a long time to collect in all my junglies, who were scattered over a couple of hundred miles but yesterday we were all together: rice by the sackful disappeared; four goats 'had it'; the most amazing variety of vegetables went into the pot and the boys stuffed themselves silly – and washed down with lashings of rum which I swear never touched the sides.

It took just half an hour's steady (very steady) drinking to provide seventeen 'stiffs' – a liberal 10% – and a good time was had by all. I'd inveigled the new

OC away from his half of the company and somehow, he managed to switch from gin to Scotch halfway through and boy- did that party swing!

We introduced our black heathens to the conga (those who could walk) and as a special finale the old man and I did a beautiful 'Hands, Knees and Boomps-a-Daisy' which creased the rest of the crowd and doubled this morning's sick parade.

It IS peacetime!!
9-09-45

It is peacetime – I've proved it!

This morning, by ignoring all pleas and protests from my orderly from 6 am onwards I stayed in bed, blissfully contemplating my toes until 8 am and then by sheer urge forced myself to gaze into the lad's black 'pans' at 9.30.

Enough – I called it a day and tried to relax but a pay parade intervened.

After lunch I thought I'd regain that Sunday peacetime feeling and was just testing the bed to see if it could take a mid-day shock when in rolls an NCO to tell me that my wagons were playing Italians!

Two of them had scuttled themselves in mud until only the tops of the wheels were showing and the drivers said, 'What do we do?'. My head is bowed in shame, I must admit – I told 'em!

Bully bombing again

Now, for the one and only news item this week. I've been 'Bully Bombing' again and it was better than ever.

Bombing is just about right as on our last circuit we put a sack of rice clean through the roof of the only hut within miles!

Have you ever 'been up'? If not, you really must – soon too – I'd never flown on such a day – the ground was blotted out by one big blanket of cloud – but up above – coo, it was simply marvellous.

The sun was shining on the snowy blanket beneath and on a single peak, which stuck up through the clouds like a cherry on a vanilla ice-cream. We pushed out the parachutes and sacks up in the mountains near the Siam border – the first 'drop' to those particular clients for a week, so I guess they forgave us the damage to their hut.

A warning – don't go into a big plane that's going to do stunts and try to stand on its tail – you'll leave your tummy behind sure and certain; I only went back for mine just in time!

PART 6

Restoring Order and Returning Home

September 1945 – July 1946

Major D.A. Townsend 1946

CHAPTER 23

Restoring Order to a Damaged Land

September '45 – February '46

Introduction:

With celebrations of the Japanese surrender now over, a new phase had begun. Restoring things to 'normality' was however going to take a long time. Japanese occupation and continual warfare for more than three years had turned Burma into a very troubled land.

On a more personal note you might well have got the impression, rightly, from more recent letters, that after years 'at the sharp end' Dad was at last beginning to get tired of his role in tank transport. A second significant factor also influenced his thinking: with peace declared, there was no longer a ban on specialist subalterns getting promoted.

As you will read in the coming section, more with a change of role than a promotion in mind, Dad had vented his feelings in a letter to the Colonel – and it was not long before that letter resulted in a very positive change.

The letters now continue:

Address: TOUNGOU GAOL
16-09-45

S'right, Towny's in Toungou – I can tell all – just halfway up Burma if you turn left at the traffic lights in Rangoon, when they are installed!

But it is quite straight – I am not <u>in</u> the gaol, I live just outside and it is the best I can do in the way of a 'civvy' address, seeing as how I go 'all civvy' on Sundays, even into combing my hair!

Let me tell you how it happened.

A month ago, I sent off a peach letter to 'Higher Authorities' explaining:

a. I seemed to be chairman of the Permanent Subalterns Club;
b. I'd stuck with my blighters whilst we were on ops, as If I hadn't either they or I would have been all shot up;
c. That I'd given the new OC time to settle down;
d. What the hell! and Pronto!!

Well, since then I've been filling up forms at about a ream a week and in a very short while, will either be a Sepoy, Air Chief Marshall or Lieut residing in either Tokyo, The Glasshouse – Aldershot or Taungou.

My but I was proud of that letter!

My duties
That very leading question on "What d'you do now, there's nothing to do?" Mmmm. When did I last write – last Sunday 9th? The week went like this:

Monday, I found myself a 'Member of a Court of Enquiry'! A lot of coolies had started to pinch some pretty coloured cloth bags from the ammo depot: the bags happened to contain cordite; one of the civilians happened to be smoking.

The seventeen I visited in hospital didn't look so good and the eight dead not even as good as that. It took the court three days to collect all the facts and record an opinion, by which time one of my own lads had swiped a Jap sword from a Burman and I had to collect the griff for his court-martial.

In between times I was doing the usual job of operating 70 trucks and 150 thugs. Which should bring us to **Thursday** – are you still with me?

On thinking it over, Thursday was a pretty tricky day – the 6.30 am PT creased me as usual and after breakfast I thought I'd visit Company HQ, miles away, to see what was cooking. I wanted to be practical, the OC wanted to be technical – our workshop went plain hysterical – I returned at 3pm for a very late and unsavoury lunch and vowed never to visit anyone, anywhere, anyhow, ever again!

Friday, I stayed at home. I gazed despondently at the wagons which wouldn't tick and crawled all over the place, thoroughly covered in grease until I was happy again.

Inspired late in the day I thought it time our September hooch ration appeared, so I went to trace it. Success! I collected on behalf of everyone but half an hour later the OC appeared looking grim. Apparently, he had thought of it too and had collected some nasty looks for asking for the stuff I'd already taken!

Yesterday I went fishing – no fish though it doesn't matter. Today I've been up the Maruchi Road and it wasn't until I was 30 miles up in the mountains that I remembered the Japs were at milestone 50 – but I did have a butterfly net!! That accounts for the enclosure.

It's now 10 pm – I was paying the boys 'til 7.30 and then made a list of tomorrows jobs: – (1) Barbers allowance (2) Barbers tools (3) Ramula – lost pay book (4) Drunk Subramanian (5) Hire civvy tailor, dhobi, sweeper (6) Cancel petrol depot night duty (7) Whisky and Gin for workshops (8) collect bug spray (9) Defective arms (10) Grease guns (11) No action A Platoon court martial (12) Hand over wagons to D Pl (13) Oil changes (14) Macaroni, cornflour, Three Nuns, Grape Nuts (15) Promote 3 L/Naiks.

There – start another war quick or better still – send a boat!!

Sport's Day
23-09-45
Aw, death warmed up means nothing to me at present – aspirins, sympathy, noggins, cooling hands upon dewy brows, ooooo-er – I need 'em all, a quick – what have I done to deserve this.

I'll leave the old body to vivisectionists, taxidermists, Salvation Army or Seventh Day Adventists – in fact anybody can have it to save me the aches and pains. It's as you'd say – much too much!

In a much-regretted moment I agreed to take the Old Man's suggestion to have a Sports Day and being the only other officer at present the OM say's 'OK Chum – you fix it!'

I fixed as ordered and then took my own two platoons' entrants into serious training all week during the 6.30–7.30 PT period.

I invite you to imagine me creeping round at daybreak teaching my lads how to start a race, how to pass a baton in relay races, how to pass the baby in all other cases, long jump, high jump and other atrocities.

Well to make a long story longer it happened yesterday – it came orf – although I've a vague feeling I was either used by the tug-o-war team as a rope or someone 'putt' me instead of a shot.

The heathens loved it – they cheered and clawed and dug fingers in each other's eyes, war danced, walked over each other and threw each other away with delight.

The last thing I'm positive about is that they tried to 'chair' me. What happened then – maybe someone offered them a free round of drinks – 'cos everyone let me go at once and whizzed off – ugh!!

OCTOBER '45

Promoted!
7-10-45

Take my free postal course in ninety easy lessons: 'write nasty letters the Towny way', results guaranteed or money back. Look what it's done for me!

That 'orrid letter I penned a while back has had results – I'm posted and now own the flowery title of STATION STAFF OFFICER, TAUNGOU – will collect another pip during the week.

New address is.

Capt D.A. Townsend, RIASC, HQ No 1, FAMO, SEAC

It's a senior office job and covers everything from birth to death – I've now got GRACIE FIELDS on my hands (I'm disposing of tickets for her show – incidentally I've given myself one!), two corpses for disposal, a committee meeting tomorrow, and I have to know the answers to everything – and I do too – try me?

Money and more besides
16-10-45

And now to come to the goings on of the Bushwhackers Union – this week I've made gifts of land, dealt with deaths of two people, one suicide and the other misguidedly fell down a well.

Yesterday I really did reflect on <u>permanent</u> retirement – I came home with Rs 193,000, which is quite a lot, about £14,000 but my bodyguards took their jobs seriously and I actually reached 'home'.[26]

The greatest recorded effort on my part was to produce a piano for a visiting concert party – I feel justified in saying that it's the only decent piano in central Burma! I nearly asked for it back halfway through their half-rate show though to give it back to the owner.

---

26 On the subject of 'money' it's worth pointing out here that currency in Burma was issued in the name of the Japanese Government from the Allies defeat in May 1942 until later on in 1945. It took a little while for these notes to be declared worthless and to be replaced initially by Indian Rupees and later by Burmese Rupees (1948) and Kyats (1952).

Pips arrive
20-10-45

This really is a peach of a job, a nice big table and a telephone and a comfortable soapbox to sit on – the box for the clients isn't so good so they don't stay long (I've a folding stool for my pals who come to chat over char!). In half an hour this morning I had to provide a building for a civil maternity clinic, two bull dozers and the answer to an awful query about hair-cutting allowance. Where's the connection?

See how I signed myself off this week? I'm back at the stage where you have to look every few minutes to see that your shoulders haven't dropped off!

Offsetting my pleasure comes the news that release of all officers has been deferred for 3 months – not so good as this means another monsoon to be waded through!

The set up
29-10-45

So, the set up. There's the Colonel (Lt Col), Australian, started this war as a conscripted private, two majors and two captains.

We've just re-decorated. Yesterday the curtains went up, so did our amazing lighting system that baffles the thousands of insects which fly around at night – and at 9.30 last night we were still splashing paint right and left.

So, believe it or not I rose at the crack of dawn (well 6.30 – it's a lovely life this) to push off the griff before the enthusiasts get cracking again. Somehow we manage to deal with all callers too, although they must be somewhat surprised at the way they are abruptly shoo-ed out of our HQ.

1200 hrs

Getting finished early didn't work, some bright guy found my phone number and pushed through a nice teaser about unexploded mines – all before breakfast too; that was followed by a crafty Burman out of contract, who was trying to supply eggs at twice the fixed price – I'll have to write between 2 and 3 am in future.

NOVEMBER '45

A strange request
4-11-45

Nothing much apart from work is happening at present – the odd Colonel drops in and baffles all of us and we pop out to the odd flick – but I must tell you this one so's when I come out of gaol you'll understand.

It was yesterday afternoon – I was chair-borne when in walks this Lt Colonel who burbles: "Come with me old man, I want to change my area" (just like that, no kid).

Off we buzz in his jeep until we come to a beautiful solid piece of jungle and he says:

'Can I have this?' 'Sure' says Towny – 'As much as you want'.

'Ok, but I'll have to knock it flat to put my battalion in'.

That knocked me kinda flat as I'm not sure how much of Burma I can give away before someone finds out – so big-hearted like I've asked the local civi big pot – he doesn't think I can give away any more at all but agreed to this one occasion.

Proper cramping my style he is!

A visit to prison
11-11-45

I really don't like admitting it, but I've been to gaol – it happened the very next day after my last letter.

The sub-area Commander, a chubby, stubby little Colonel visited us, and I had to show him around the town. We were passing the civvy gaol, a lovely piece of work which puts all Granadas in the shade for commissionaires and ornamentation (no usherettes though) and he shouts out: "Whoa we're going in here."

I thought that someone must have delivered my letter to him instead of you but no, all we did was swarm up and down stairs and ladders and things gaze at 'lifers' and watch the efforts of hard labourers and away we went.

I'm reformed though – never more will I swipe someone else's beer or take a chaps last fag –leastways not until tomorrow!

Meeting Pete Rees himself!

Buy me a size larger hat, will you? If I go on at the present rate my head is due to burst. I haven't washed my hand this week, not since Pete Rees came puffing up the stairs and was introduced all round.

He said, "I haven't met you have I" so I gave him "Yes, on the Stiletto Column" [*this was the first column into Mandalay*] and left it at that – you can't very well remind a General that he'd told you to get your wagons moving when the PBI were only just in front winkling out the Japs.

Anyway, he opened out and gave us all the whole story over again – it's one of his favourites as he wasn't supposed to pull off that stunt anyway.

Nowadays he goes round Toungou on a horse (it was hitched up outside when he was with us) because he doesn't like the Jap prisoners to see how small a man he is.

Cinema owner and high-class tea!
18-11-45

Meet Alexander Goldstein, Gaumont Waldorf Towny Inc – I own two cinemas!

Free gifts from the Gods and I can do what I like with 'em – cor if I could understand Tamil and Hindi, I'd go every night. Bring your own seat, shoes, opera glasses and hot water bottle and free entertainment is yours – at a price!

That aside, this afternoon I was invited out to tea by the Burmese owner of the house we live in. He's a nice old boy, silver-haired, speaks excellent English, knows more about Dickens, Thackeray, Scott, Decline and Fall and Uncle Tom's Cabin than I ever will, has some super-fine crockery recently recovered from a jungle hidey-hole: five daughters, five sons and a generous sprinkling of grandchildren, a bamboo hut and good sales talk!

I spent a couple of hours chatting and eating and discovered that: (1) Burma is far worse than Chicago or China for bandits and hold-ups and (2) when a guy becomes a corpse the body can only be buried on the 3rd, 5th, 7th or 9th day after death – which makes things hum if one of the chief mourners happens to miss the weekly bus.

Not only that, but the body has to have a sentry over it night and day, so they usually provide a party to fix up a gambling school to pass the time. I understand the gamblers often argue and generally use knives, which makes another corpse – so the great world keeps turning.

Winter Cold – and a possible trip to Indo-China!
25-11-45
Well chum, all the stone and brass Buddhas in the temple have now started hugging themselves 'cos it's so cold.

Naturally they've always sat there with hands wrapped round their knees, but I never realised why – if only there were fireplaces included when Burmese houses were built. And when I brave the unknown by dashing from my charpoy at 6.30 prompt, the little idol that graces my room gives a wicked grin with a 'you've had it chum' kinda look.

I thought, when I came into this job, after all that wandering o'er the countryside, that it would be peaceful, roses blooming by the wayside and Towny surrounded by phones, glass topped table and er – well no, the dumb blonde typists weren't expected but – well.

Fact is that it's not like that at all –halfway through this week the boss had a message telling him to send another chap and I to Indo-China to run an airstrip.[27] I mean to say – it's a trifle unsettling to have a thing like an airstrip given to one at no extra cost whatsoever.

Still, as things are at present, we are <u>not</u> going but there's no telling when the upper crust will find some other place for us to go – maybe even more remote.

DECEMBER '45

Railway Connected
2 -12-45
Now what's happened here since I last poured out the 'gen'. Ah yes indeed – a booze ration has arrived that's priority A1 +++ and so's the railway. So have hundreds and hundreds of jungly Indians and Burmese who have to be housed.

I'm due to go to the flicks tonight to see *Burma Victory* just to get an idea of what really happened. Who said, "I was there and how!!!!"

I've been wandering o'er wastelands again – plodding round native villages with a guide, checking if, when and how long the military occupied the houses.

---

27 F.A.M.O, the organisation that Dad now worked for, stands for 'Forward Airfield Maintenance Organisation'. As well as being responsible for restoring local civil order in Burma they were also responsible for 'Forward' Airfields all over Indo-China.. 'Forward' in this context meant they were part of 'forward operations' near the enemy.

Although 'peace' was now declared in Burma there was still unrest in many other areas and these bases were still being used for military supplies. Not a good place to go to!

It's quite a good job as long as the folks are pleasant – I've had some very odd brews of tea in poky little bamboo huts, while in other places the folks manage to produce the last three cups and saucers and a tablecloth.

19 Division Tattoo – a real good do
8-12- 45
We went to the 19 Division Tattoo last night, a real good do of about 18 items with lots of half pint size Ghurkhas jogging around as tin soldiers, Africans doing terrifying war dances, Pathans kinda sharpening their knives for next year's war against us and bags of Generals and things hanging around.

We've had one of our own G's staying with us, plus the Colonel from Sub-Area, who treats the room next to mine as his country residence every time he gets browned off with work 150 miles away.

As I was saying – the Div put on a good show which nearly compensated us for the trouble they caused since they first thought of the thing.

Another Change of Role
The week's joke – I was posted to a 'Graves Registration and Concentration Unit' in the middle of that flap I mentioned – and I refused to go – another stooge volunteered and so I'm now SSO [*Station Staff Officer*] no longer but **Adjutant FAMO** – a nice job too.

JANUARY '46

1-1-46

Festivities and the Colonel's despatch
I report that the fittest have survived and still remain fit (for nothing). I'll begin by recounting our own quiet affairs!

To begin with I'll have to work backwards as I can still remember fairly clearly what happened this morning – the Colonel left on route for Australia.

We had gone to bed at 4.30 am – I'll get to that later – and for reasons unknown I was up at 8.15 (today is a holiday).

At nine o'clock twelve people came in for breakfast. I decorated the CO's jeep with 3 signboards, old boots, bottles, tin cans and a bunch of bananas and decked the whole thing out with flags, whilst the lads organised our convoy – 11 jeeps!!

No 1 was loaded with an air-raid siren and a case of beer, No 2 was a motor-cycle out rider, the cheer leader armed with a Jap sword came in No 3: the old boy himself with a sister (Q A) perched on the back, came next and I led the rest as a choir (God rest their souls!).

We toured Toungou first and gave 19 Div a shock from which it will never recover and then escorted Digger to the town boundary: had a beer session and gave a final salute with every pistol and tommy gun we could muster.

We are now in mourning as his going is a sad loss and he'll be hard to replace. Bill, our major who is officiating CO has gone to Rangoon for three days leaving me to hold a huge armful of babies, dozens of the ruddy little things which all seem to kick and squirm at the same time.

New Years' Eve party

Going back into the dim mists of time I also recall, after a busy day of giving people back their homes, our New Year's Party starting at about 8 pm.

It developed, that's just about all I can say – it developed and went with such a swing that by mid-night our numbers were halved, and our voices gone completely.

We then, with our three Aberdonians and two very 'low' Scots, proceeded to maintain the tradition of 'visiting'. Taking our own bottles, we made the rounds, visiting people we knew, people who knew us, people we've never seen and people who never want to see us again.

Phew, I was acting as chauffeur to the Colonel and so only drank two to his three but my, oh my, I remember we visited our own mess on three separate occasions during the night, the last time simply because we were going up a road and saw a light shining. We went upstairs to find some of the gang operating the bar as if they owned it, so we let them carry on and joined in!

Happy New Year from the locals

Before all this occurred, we had a very touching moment – seated fairly quietly in our mess before any of the foregoing hostilities commenced, we were each presented with a letter addressed to ourselves in the best copperplate and a terrific bunch of bananas was hoisted on to the table.

The owner of our house, the old boy, who lives in his new bamboo hut next door, and his family, were wishing us a Happy New Year and on each greeting was pinned a silver peacock broach.

Well – I assure you we did feel things, living in a chap's house when he does things like that!

Previous festivities – now recounted.
Also 1-1-46

I'm now going to go way back as far as I can (to the last time I was really sober) and 'gen' you up to date.

Trouble is to remember where to begin – I've sent separately a copy of the operation order I published and distributed to all the units in Toungou and that started officially on Christmas Eve but, as far as I know, someone slipped a crafty party on the 23rd which was not on the agenda.

All our parties are the same, 20–30 men, 2 or 3 sisters from the hospital, so games and dancing are almost impossible. We sing, then the girls go home, and we sing louder and er – louder until either the voices are gone, or the bar is dry.

Christmas Day '45

A cloudless, warm day and the air like crystal after the fug in which we'd been the night before. I spent part of the morning padding around the native bazaar, looking in vain for prawns (freshwater variety). All I got was a variety of odd smells, so we broke it up and came home to serve up dinner for the BORs [*British Other Ranks*].

The BOR's Christmas Lunch

There were four officers and six sergeants on parade, to wait upon eight others (the ninth was 'out' but put up a good show later on) so the service was 'Par excellence'.

So was the food – it should be as we feed the 15,000 troops in the area and they all did well. Frozen duck, pork and ham was something out of the bag specially sent up from a 'frig' ship in Rangoon and all-in large quantities too.

I won't go on – we tiptoed away to leave the lads at the table where they lay gasping, to face our own feast. We too had done very well indeed: the contractor from whom all the supplies are bought came along with a goose, three ducks, an iced cake and a lot of fresh veg: oooh how we saw them off!

The party that night

The party was to be at our place that night, so I had to whip up some snappy decorations with a rush. Flowers everywhere, in wall vases (loaned from the old boy next door) and vari-tinted balls of cotton wool strung out across the room and also cotton wool 'snow' dripping from our pictures, changed the face of the place considerably and all went smoothly.

That night I almost touched the 'bottle opening' record at one time but we've changed all that now. Everyone has to carry their own opener around and produce it when demanded by the doorman.

Boxing Day

Boxing Day was a shamble. Bill [*the Major*] found his way into the bulk canteen depot where all the liquor stocks are kept. He climbed to the top of the large pile of beer filled sacks, lay flat on his back and proceeded to drink as many as he could as fast as he could: disposing of the empties over his shoulder in Henry VIII fashion!

The party that night was therefore something else!

My old Coy – 164, is breaking up and that night we helped them on their way. What a do! A Jeep was driven through the mess tent (someone was climbing over the roof at the time), the jungle was lit up with Verey Lights, a fireplace knocked flat and we ended up with a pipe of peace around a log fire.

The 27th

A rather wan Towny staggered into his office on the 27th, gazed at his two trays marked 'after Xmas' and 'New Year' and did his best to demolish the piles of piffle therein.

That night we attended a Karen concert [*the Karen people form a significant element of the Burmese nationals*] – in the open and the cold – very good for us too and gave us a good night to come back to normal. The native dancing and music were enough to sober up the best of the bad types.

28th

Our Sergeants invited us to their mess on the *28th* with one intention only – to see us under the table: we ended up 4 to 2 in our favour, every officer returning to base and 5 sgts out for the count. I've really got cotton wool legs now – must be soaking up the gubbins somehow!

Now it's all over and I promise to be good and quiet – at least for the moment – must go steady y'know, group 31 will turn up any month now [*'Group 31' was his allotted group for sailing home*].

Winding Down
5-01-46

Y'know in a few days' time, when 19 Div have completely left there will only be about 21 British Officers in Taungou and 7 sisters in the hospital. The social whirl will no longer be a dashing affair.

To prove how much reformed, I am I attended a flick last night, *Fanny by Gaslight*. It <u>was</u> cold in the open but very enjoyable for all that (we postponed the start of the film for half an hour because our bath water was late in being prepared) – pretty good to control a cinema isn't it!

Trouble from Dacoits[28]

Apart from that essay into the wide-open spaces to see the flick, we usually stay at home at night: these dacoit guys are becoming more of a menace than a nuisance-— three robberies in the middle of the town last night and this afternoon 164 copped a packet from a raving band who had knives and grenades and two of the lads, the mess cook and waiter, were killed.

I'm telling you, when it was only the Japs, we were up against we had a rough idea where to find them: – now the chap who lives across the street might be a night bird for all we know – they are here, there and everywhere!

I'm now going into training for the boat and can almost count days (a lot of them I know) 'til I climb aboard.

Back to the Day Job
13-01-46

In anticipation of the job, I hope to do – I mean giving away what is not mine – I donated a large lump of jungle to a Jap Prison camp, only to find that I'd picked the only piece of leased ground within fifty miles.

All this week I've been dashing around (as much as I ever do dash) collecting the landowners OK and placing ice upon the brow of the little guy who calls himself 'Superintendant of Land Records' who says I should have asked him first!

Still, we're matey again and I've been asked out to tea – he said "Come round to meet my daughters" – so it looks as if I start this week with having to placate him all over again!

---

28 Dacoits is the name in Burma and India for a member of a band of armed robbers.

Area Commander Coming to Inspect
20-01-46

Y'know, if any other so and so dares salute me today I'll throw a fit!

As our area commander is coming to inspect Taungou next week I thought I'd have a crafty tour myself today to work out the answers. Ugh, I started at our Jap POW camp and finished there too!

There are a thousand Nips in occupation and I'm sure every one of them saluted me twice and – as I'm meant to be 'coldly courteous and return all compliments punctiliously' (what a language!) – I'm now suffering from a sprained wrist.

A thousand odd Japs and I saw seven IORs [*Indian Other Ranks*] sitting talking – they were the guards. I was met by a Jap major who kowtowed, whistled up an interpreter and showed me round.

Very nice place too – considering it was solid jungle two weeks ago. Now we have japs riding around on mo'bikes, driving cars, issuing our rations, wandering all over the place un-escorted and generally having quite a reasonable time.

It won't be long before they out number us and I wouldn't be surprised if we didn't send them out against the decoits! What a place this is!

Some light relief

May I recommend home movies to you – we had our private show last Monday and it was super. FAMO's 'Monday Night at Eight' we called it and providing the new films arrive in time we mean to continue it each week. It is really most essential that it continues as now our petrol is rationed our recreational trips are reduced to a minimum.

FAMO to break up soon
26-01-46

The stars foretell that FAMO is to break up very soon and maybe Towny will terrorise Toungou no more. I'm hoping I can stick around as I'm quite happy to await the boat in comfort.

Promoted to Major!!

Though there is no mention in the content of the letters of his promotion, all letters from 26th January '46 give Dad's rank as 'Major'.

This supports what his sister Shirley had always told me "He was one of the youngest majors in the Indian Army." I guess, as he was still only 25½, that has a good chance of being true.

FEBRUARY '46

3-02-46

Crazy Communications!

I have just had an official letter to say that FAMO must disband from effect **1st Nov '45** which makes it appear that the last three months work has only been a mirage, a nasty dream or a pain in the neck.

It also looks as if yours most untruly is going to have a bit of a job to find out what job he has been doing since 1 Nov and what rank and cash go with it – I'm <u>most</u> interested!

There's a new Colonel arriving this afternoon so I'm just off to prune the moustache, so he'll see me when he gets here.

Two letters are missing but, by deduction, after his promotion he was transferred to a town called Pegu. This is 100 miles south of Toungou, around 40 miles north of Rangoon (now Yangon). Today Pegu is known as Bago.

Five aces
28-02-46

I'm awfully sorry I'm so late this time but things have been kinda flapping recently and I've been dashing to and from Rangoon each day to take evidence for a court martial (No – not mine – yet).

Now, meet the most unpopular man in Pegu. Do you know of or play poker dice? – you shouldn't but anyway I'm the guy who threw five aces last night and cleared the jackpot! Tonight, we've all to go to the flicks as the rest of the boys are broke.

No news on the leave as yet.

MARCH '46
5-03-46

Back to Toungou

Being big hearted to myself I went to Toungou for the weekend to see all the boys I left behind (incidentally to do the odd atom of work too but I don't kid myself).

It was a very nice break and we disturbed about half the population of Burma by returning in 31/2 hours for 126 miles, which meant that most of the time we were doing over 50 mph. Why this letter isn't being written on a piece of cloud I can't understand; we didn't hit anything, but a lot of people won't have to go to the barber for a shave this week!

Leaving in around 10 weeks

I've only just realised that I won't be writing to you much longer – I should be leaving in about 10 weeks.

Tell me, while there is still time – what is your phone number? Towny's Tours Unlimited will arrange an international hook-up on receipt of this most important information and at least give you a tinkle from the port of dis-embarkation.

So, per-lease don't be surprised if, when you lift the phone, you hear a noise like a traffic accident – that'll be my voice!

And there the letters end. At least there are no more letters recorded. The next written record is the diary of the trip home which now follows.

CHAPTER 24

The Diary of the Trip Home

May – July 1946

Introduction

With Dad's unit, 'FAMO', being disbanded in January '46 it was at last time for him to start thinking about getting home. He was not alone; many servicemen were in a similar position and there appears to be no preference given by rank or length of service. So, despite having been recently promoted to Major and having been abroad for five years without a break, the wait was to be a long one.

The diary starts in May. The first entry is made when Dad is in a military camp near Calcutta, having just had some leave. His first task is to get a boat back from there to Rangoon and then to get a boat home. The boat he eventually gets from Rangoon leaves on the 14th June, six years almost to the day since he signed up on his birthday on 13th June 1940.

*The diary now follows, copied exactly as it was written. The only additions are in italics and occasional **bold** print to pick out the main places and events.*

THIS IS IT – JUST AS IT WAS WRITTEN:

May 12th '46: Reported Barackpore [*a city in West Bengal near Calcutta – Kolkata*] **Transit Camp** – about 50th on list for passage to Rangoon. 3 weeks stay probable.

Mon 13/5: Nothing

Tues 14/5: Took trunk to be crated and spent day in Calcutta.

Wed 15/5: Nothing! 11 from top of list to leave on 17th – I'm going to try to fix in on that boat.

FRI 14th June '46:

British Transit Camp, Rangoon. Up at 04.30. Washed, shaved and packed up in the dark. First drafts assembled at 05.45 on a fine but cloudy morning. We can only take on the boat what we can carry ourselves and many people left behind boxes, bedding and minor items of personal belongings.

I helped a couple of chaps by stowing a bottle of whisky and a sheet in my spare space. We loaded our bags on to a jeep trailer and pushed it down to the assembly point. A patient wait, we moved off in a lorry at 0715. A final glimpse of THE EAST from the back of the truck – was quite a good cross section – Indians, Burmese, Chinese, the Shwedagon pagoda [*also known as the Golden Dragon Pagoda – the most sacred Buddhist Pagoda in Myanmar*] rickshaws, bicycles, and ancient buses, nice smells, horrible stinks.

A hot and sticky wait at the docks delayed us until 0815 when, with much grunting and groaning, too heavy kits were hauled on to a flat lighter towed by a dirty tug. Circled in the river, chugged down passed the few ships anchored at quay and in-stream and down along the Rangoon waterfront – the city to port, the few huts and bazaars on the flat starboard side. Our ship the ***ORDUNA*** is anchored about three miles downstream. Two miles are covered, and a monsoon storm sweeps across the estuary causing all the rigging cleats to flap like a broody hen. I donned a cape and sat over my two grips as if I was hatching them – those who had hoped to defy the monsoon were soaked.

As we pulled alongside, the rain stopped and we were left to watch the antics of the unfortunates who, at the time, were tackling the gang plank – and hopes of many were lowered when they saw how narrow it was. My turn eventually came, and I didn't like it – my bags became heavier and heavier and I felt sure that I'd drop one as the blxxdy staircase swayed. I made it and was met by a mass of people all travelling in ever decreasing circles – we reported to the purser's office and each was given a ticket showing where he or she was to sleep. Dormitory B2 didn't sound bad to me.

I found B deck OK and then dormitory No 2 – but really it couldn't be right, it was full to overflowing already with bunks three deep and people clambering over them in search of either air or kit – the former, I think! It was true though, so I launched myself into the throng to find only one of the top and most inaccessible bunks vacant and nowhere to fit my kit. I put it on someone else's and let him find a place to put it for me!

I went up on deck for air!! There were queues everywhere and I found an interesting one, which would have told me where to eat, when and with whom – as if I cared! So I found Bill Rose and asked him to fix it – and I continued to watch people embark; much more interesting, especially as an everlasting flow of women in various stages of old age were then coming on board.

At last everyone settled down – except the bloke who nattered continually over the tannoy loud speaker – W.O. [*Warrant Officer*] this, to report to orderly room; Flight Lt. this, to go to gang plank, Pte A is wanted on the mess deck; all Indian Army Officers to bring form H(i) (ii) to Ship Office at once – Christ, that means me!!!

It all worked out, everyone had a place for lunch, and food with it! At 1200, after a minor flap while the soon to be – ex governor of Burma, Sir Whatsit Dorman Smith [*Colonel Sir Reginald Hugh Dorman Smith was Governor of Burma from 6/5/41 to 31/08/46 – now on his way back to retire*] came aboard, we sailed, and all was excitement. I then ventured below to the bunkhouse – jeese was it crammed – and decided not to do a thing until I had to.

Washing water is on from 0600–0800, 1730–1830 – looks as if I'll have to powder instead of bathing. A general tour of exploration followed – including adding to the number of Officers I already knew, the number of VADs [*Voluntary Aid Detachment – a unit of civilians providing nursing care for military personnel*], WAS(B's) [*Women's Auxiliary Service (Burma) – 250 volunteers providing canteen services to troops in Burma*] and QA's [*Queen Alexandra's Royal Army Nursing Corp*] who I hoped I'd never know.

At 1600 came a practice of emergency stations – a shambles, so everyone was happy.

Queues for tea, for washing, to look over the side, followed but as I don't like queues I find it easier to wait and take my time. Dinner was at 1800 after collecting real £ in place of our Indian and Burmese currency. After that I simply put myself out to air over the rail and spent the evening talking – good sales talk as I won a bob at liar dice! Clocks went back ½ hr and I went to bed!

SAT 15th June

I don't know what day this is so I'll fill it in later. Up at 0645 to catch the washing water. Being an early time for meals I'd finished breakfast by 0815 and again put myself out to air over the rail with a pipe. Isabel West joined me and left again. 5 mins later one of loves young dreams came along and asked me where 'Timber' had gone – I told her so she stayed talking to me for an hour; things must be bad when the girls can't get hooked up in the normal way. Still, we can always raise our hats, say 'good morning' and pass on.

Boat stations at 1000 wasted another 45 mins. Only another 26–28 days to waste and we'll be home. Rumour has it that we're landing at Liverpool, after calling at possibly **Aden. Pt Said, Gibraltar**, due 14–15 July – I wish it had been the 9th or 10th.[29]

After lunch I thought I'd add a bit to that tan so decked myself out in shorts and clambered up to boat deck to find monsoon showers had sent everyone scurrying inside. I've borrowed a book of 709 pages – *Northwest Passage* – so I dip into it whenever there's nothing else to do and don't notice the difference! Ship ran a sweep on distance run -- 253 miles so far.

Spent all the evening trying to dry out of a super sweat I threw after a hurried wash before dinner. Tired for reasons unknown (maybe exposure to sea breeze) I turned in at 21.30.

SUN 16th June

My, these bunks are comfy, even if cramped. I was forced out of mine by the necessity for being in time for breakfast. Now that's a thing – the food on this boat leaves plenty to be desired and I guess if most of the folks weren't on their way 'out' and so don't wish to start trouble at this stage, there'd be plenty of complaints.

The sun appeared today and sitting on the boat deck I found I was rather lobster like by mid-day – distance run 311 miles (total 464). It couldn't continue though, and the afternoon was showery and gusty and it cooled the ship down considerably and I salt water showered while it was possible to do so without excess sweating. People still seem inclined to queue for things that cost too much anyway – I still prefer to sit back.

One of the lads shaved off his moustache this morning – conscience or a mistake with the razor? the former for a guess as his wife would have told him to 'whip it orf!'. Managed to fix a ticket for the cinema show for tonight. There are two shows, one early for the lads – Bing in *Going My Way* and ours at 2030 – *Gentleman Jim*. While waiting for the show to begin we joined in a crowd who were community singing – and enjoyed it!

---

29 10th July was the birthday of his pen-friend Connie!

The flick took place in a lounge and because of the large numbers admitted, some of us saw it from strange angles. I know I did but still it went down well and filled in a couple of hours nicely. After the show we wandered round the boat deck in the moonlight – very pleasant. I now seem to know so many of the other chaps that its useless to put down who I was with when anything special happens as usually about four of us start something and twenty end up together.

MON 17th June 46
Still going and still managing to get washed and showered before breakfast! 34 in our dormitory and only 3 wash basins – I don't know how we do it, but it seems to work out. Have made good progress with the *Northwest Passage* – in spite of continual interruption by the lads. Sunbathing early A.M. and immediately after lunch, ½ hour each day front and back and then trying to keep in the shade as much as possible. Lots of people have overdone it and are complaining of sore backs and legs and look like lobsters.

Daily run was 318 miles (782).

Tomorrow we should reach **Ceylon** and call at **Colombo** so that'll give us something to look at – it's hard to avoid monotony on a boat even if there are plenty of books to read. Weeks cigarette and tobacco rations were issued during morning – I collected 1/2lb Capstan for 4/- – pretty good.

Tombola filled up evening but no luck.

TUES 18TH June '46
Finished book soon after breakfast and then went up on boat deck to pen this. **Ceylon** has been on starboard beam all the time since we first came up on deck and we've now altered course, travelling north to Colombo.

There's a very strong swell on the sea today and the old crate has been doing all sorts of gymnastics except somersaults. Arrived off **Colombo** at 1500hrs and waited for a boat to come out of the harbour. Jeese! It was the *SAMARIA*, the ruddy old tub that first brought me from home – who'd have guessed! Looks as if she too is homeward bound.

The seas were smashing into the harbour wall and water and spray was going up about 50 ft – they say it's always like this. The pilot boat kept disappearing in the troughs while coming out to us but eventually we trickled in through the gap in the piers with the small lighthouses on the end of each. The harbour inside was pretty well packed and the battleship *Duke of York* was there with sailors on parade and a marine band playing; we thought it was for us until it became apparent that they were about to sail and were putting on the usual line of Navy tradition.

A monsoon storm and dinner time coincided to push us below, but we'd already hailed most of the vessels and gathered that the town looked alright from a distance. The harbour looked good at night – so did the surrounding land and lighted streets; considerably warmer below decks now we have no breeze entering portholes but it's going to be worse in a few days when we leave the monsoon area.

Lots of people seem to be hobbling around suffering from over exposure to the sun and some very nasty lobster colour legs are tenderly stretched as the owners murmur "never again will I sunbathe!" Taught one of the lads liar dice at night which should be a good start for him in civvy street!

Turned in early and had soon soaked my pillow with perspiration.

WEDS 19TH June

Awakened at 0645 after sleeping for about 5 minutes, or so it seemed – I sleep almost as soon as I touch down. The **Highland Princess** had berthed alongside while I wasn't looking, littered with Navy types. Spent most of the morning gazing over the side with or without the aid of binoculars – minelayer **Manxman** came in and one or two more cargo boats – a really busy port is this.

Occasional rainstorms cleared everyone off the decks, but they seem to be short and sweet. Rumour still rife about our time of departure – personally I hope it's soon. Just before lunch an aircraft carrier pulled in which, as everyone on our ship went to watch her, gave us a considerable list to starboard!

A doubtful lunch – the food has not improved – was followed by an hours 'deck quoits' and sun-bathing and an hours reading in the shade and here I am, down below at 1515, on my bunk, rain outside and sticky inside ; still in harbour unfortunately - let's get cracking. All sorts of entertainment seems to be developing: a concert, a chess tournament, tombola, morning and evening half hours of recorded music and some queer calls over the loud speakers.

Today's problem is washing oneself – yesterday fresh water was ad lib; everyone was invited to do their laundry. Most of us bashed out a few of our things and several of the lads put them out to dry on the boat deck and have left them there since – to be soaked at every shower and odd items to be blown over the side. Still while in port we can't shower with salt water as we are wont. It's a bit mucky!!

Today therefore we must sluice and hope for the best. 1600–1630 was an interesting period watching food being hauled aboard from a rickety native boat by a couple of local workers. Then we up with the anchor and leave port with quite a send-off from the *Highland Princess* next to us, who had disembarked all the Navy bodies and seemed to have only a few civilians left.

Reading after dinner and teaching another chap liar dice. Before bed spent half an hour on the boat deck on what seemed to be a half gale. Lots of swell and the boat pitches and tosses in a big way.

Approx 40 miles since noon on 18/6

THURS 20th June

Only ready just in time for breakfast – I like a nice soft bunk with a gentle rolling motion. Sunbathing, rain dodging, boat stations, reading, sunbathing and it was soon lunch time. After that I began a queue for a haircut, electric clippers and all mod cons, feel a lot better for it too. A saltwater shower to clean up as best as possible and now once again I'm in my bunk at 1500, writing this when everyone else seems to be asleep.

Later – I slept! A thing I rarely do and do not like as I awake feeling like death warmed up. Still, it passes the time which is the bigger problem.

Heat set in after dinner and the evening seemed interminable. Today's mileage was 235, since sailing last night until midday. Total now approx 1463

FRI 21st June

One week aboard and it seems a lifetime but in other ways has passed quickly – strange but true. Fine weather, mostly with plenty of time for sunbathing but odd showers make everyone scurry for cover. Boat stations at 1000 – a regular occurrence except on Sundays and when in port. Many people suffering from too much sun and I'm told a baby has been born today – quick work!!

Monotony has set in and books aren't quite enough to pass the time. Sunned ourselves whilst playing deck quoits but at the same time became dirty and sticky – there's always a catch in it some place.

Miles 290. Started chess playing to pass time – and it does! Made some instant purchases from canteen – shaving gear, nail scissors and razor – may avoid comments back home. There is still a heavy swell on the sea and we pitch and toss all over the place.

SAT 22ND June

Out in the sun all the morning, which may or may not be a good thing an
will have to judge by results. Played chess on deck till lunch time, worst hazar
being the wind which sweeps down the deck as the ship buries her nose int
the seas. We are no longer required on boat stations, leaving us another ha
hour to fill for ourselves. These are lazy days and will continue to be so unt
we have something to look at in the Red Sea – all we have now is miles an
miles of water day after day. Tombola at 2000 hrs – completely unsuccessfu
and hardly raised a sweat of excitement – must recoup losses next time or els

Mileage 280 – even slower, as we are going dead into the wind and seas an
will do so until out of the monsoon area, any day now, I hope. Although the
we are going to be a trifle hot!

SUN 23rd June

Got up with a rush as I'd forgotten to put back my watch ½ hour last nigh
and so thought I was late for breakfast – it all worked out alright though an
I was in time. Brekker included frozen apples which went down a treat. Firs
ship we've seen since Colombo is an aircraft carrier coming up on the [por
– *crossed out*] starboard stern: maybe my nautical terms are haywire but that
where the boat is anyway.

Later announced that it was the **Rajah,** Colombo – Aden, and then anothe
passed going the other way – the seas full of 'em!

Slept in afternoon and suffered for it as at night, couldn't sleep quite as we
– but I put up a pretty good imitation. 270 miles only covered.

MON 24th June

Both yesterday and today have had some of the roughest seas yet – there mus
be 50–60ft movement at the bow and stern and now and again the whol
caboodle shudders as we crash into a huge wave and the sea breaks down ove
the lower decks and sprays all the rest. We've had to close the portholes of ou
dormitory (34 of us in a normal peace time 4–6 berth cabin) and even the
the water comes in through a sky light. Today mileage was only 230, agains
a terrific wind (a gale I suppose) and all the waves which seem to be going th
other way.

I can't write straight as I'm being pushed around all over the place by th
sway of the boat. A morning of sunbathing, an afternoon of reading and chess
five days from **Columbo** and we're still at least 3 days short of **Aden.** Fres

water has been cut down as we're running short in view of the additional time which will be necessary to reach Suez. Spent last evening doing some washing which has turned out ok and I've now brought out my battle dress for airing and de-creasing.

At night in lounge, a small band, piano, uke and 2 accordions keep us well entertained, with us singing –? in unison or harmony. Still, it makes the time pass quickly and was much appreciated.

TUES 25th June

Made a complete mess of things early this morning as the clocks had gone back 30 mins and I didn't know it – was up far too early and had to lounge around wasting time in consequence. At 0845 hrs we came to the end of the monsoon – just like that! At any rate the clouds disappeared, the sea, which had been buffeting us for several days, calmed down and we were left with a clear blue sky, blazing sun, howling wind and a gentle pitch and toss of the boat. Sunbathing as there is no alternative – everyone does it.

Daily run 261 miles – proof of the easier going this morning, should now improve daily. Afternoon was spent in horse racing – backed winners in 1st and 2nd races but thereafter was unsuccessful and ended up 2/- down. No books left in the ships library so was forced to watch chess players after dinner and came to the decision that perhaps my chess is not so bad after all. Bed early 20.30.

WEDS 26th June

Awakened by stuffiness of dormitory, excess sweating and muzzy head – portholes were shut owing to spray and sea blowing into our windward (port) side and got out as soon as possible to write this. First case of things to come – I imagine the wind will now be a hot one, the sea calmer and the sun in a cloudless sky, terrific – but it will have nice sunsets!

Heard yesterday that the old tub has her bow full of concrete, having staved in the plating in Singapore some time back – hence we can't crash into the seas but must let them hit us – very nice too!

Written 27/6 Sky remained overcast for large part of the day but even so people reddened more than usual. Sea calm and wind modest. At 1130 – after boat stations, **locusts started landing on this ship** – dozens of them, pink 21/2 – 31/2 inches long.

Chess on deck all pm and same again in evening. At night, as it is so hot below, spent some time sitting on deck doing nothing. Clocks back 30 minutes. Mileage covered 304.

THURS 27th June

Very hot below decks at night and sleeping became uncomfortable. Rose early and cooled off on deck. Locusts, which travelled with us yesterday, now mostly gone. 0800 land in sight to east **(Yemen – Arabia)** 09.30 **Aircraft Carrier Formidable** passed, 2 1/2 miles away travelling south. 1000hrs we overtook a Portuguese motor assisted sailing vessel (4 masts) which ran up a flag signal, which was afterwards found out to be 'pleasant voyage'- nice of them – we hooted back.

Land both sides and we passed **Perim Island** and into **the Red Sea** at 1200 hrs. Keeping out of the sun for a bit as its silly to overdo things and a surprising number of people are being treated for sunburn. Castor oil limited activities!. Kept to C Deck, one above ours, for the rest of the day – getting intensely hot at night and everyone perspiring profusely.

2000hrs **Empress of Scotland**, Bombay – Southampton overtook us travelling fast. Later heard she was originally **Empress of Japan** – a ship in the convoy in '41 – certainly looked the same. Clocks back 30 minutes. Mileage 318.

FRI 28th June

Up at 0115 – 0445 – partly owing to the extreme heat: soaked bedding with perspiration. Stayed up at 0445 and went on deck to cool off, watch sunrise and watch porpoises keeping up with the boat. A baby one tore along with mother and jumped out of the water when she did – pretty to watch.

Yesterday afternoon, while hanging over rail, knocked out word picture of Red Sea and surrounds as it was at the time. Here it is:

'A dazzling vista of white and blue, good to behold but painful to the eyes.

Yellow white whispy clouds, faint grey outline of land in extreme distance, nearer at hand a grey lighthouse on white jutting rocks / perhaps two miles distant: brilliant white sails of feluccas [*a traditional wooden sailing boat in the eastern Mediterranean*] as they turn into the sun, changing to a sullen grey in the shade.

White birds against a blue green sea; white foam pushed up by the bow of the ship and being flicked off the top of the waves by the light breeze. In the distance the intriguing smoke of a vessel as yet below the horizon – is she coming or going, big or small? Mercantile or Navy?

The log, in the water, spins the indicator at the end of the boom, whilst the smaller wheel, geared down, methodically ticks off the miles. ORs [*Other ranks*] sitting, lying, sprawling on the deck, lounging against or leaning over the rail: brown bodies, well developed bodies, shining ones, spotty ones, tattooed, tanned, and tattered; the inevitable togetherness of some, for the married ones, a packet of biscuits from the canteen. The tannoy interrupts occasionally and then a programme of music is hoarsely put over. The officers' women and WOs [*Women Officers*] in the lounges or on the boat deck, many sunning themselves or struggling to keep in the shade as both the boat and the sun move on their courses. The hardy and perhaps foolish play deck tennis or deck quoits – heatstroke is easily come by.

As night draws in the deck slowly clears. People queue for showers and the fresh water in the basins. Officers and the ladies emerge spruced up and thoroughly uncomfortable for the first sitting of dinner (1800hrs) when they will descend into the depths, perspire profusely and pretend it's funny. The sun descends behind greyish clouds – unspectacular – the time for lovely sunsets is not yet.

The lights come on, bright in the lounges and recreation rooms, insufficient on the decks – the lads can't read so sit and talk and smoke. The 'blower' announces a cinema show to start at 2000 hrs and restricts attendance to specific drafts. Cards appear all over the ship – bridge for the officers and pontoon – below decks they favour solo. The women fiddle with patience, give it up and talk nothings amongst themselves or to anyone who will listen.

The ship settles down, there is no motion at all, no sense of movement unless one looks over the side, a complete contrast to the days of ups and downs and sickness on the Indian Ocean. A hush settles over the ship – hammocks and sleeping gear is strewn around the decks and small groups whisper amongst themselves rather than hold general conversations and slowly the whole assembly settle down to sleep, muttering and groaning of the heat if below decks, or to a quiet uninterrupted slumbering in a cool position on deck.

Later – wrote letter card to folks for despatch wherever we call – tells them all I know of our arrival (which isn't much). MO [*Medical Officer*] says a little food – I need it bad – weak. Mileage 323 – pretty good and most encouraging. Surface of sea is patchy with browny covering; I thought it was dust but am told it is animal matter and from it the sea derives its name (i.e.,' Red Sea') – as we say in liar dice 'it could be'!

Too hot to sunbathe or do anything but loaf around reading or hang over the side in the gentle breeze. No luck at Tombola which I had Jock play for me – I'm keeping on lower decks!

SAT 29th June

Awakened at 0345 – bunk dripping with perspiration – turned bedding over and re-awakened at 0730 only just in time for the freshwater which is turned off at that hour. Felt considerably refreshed in spite of quite a dampened sleep. Reading, crib, etc AM – doc says eat and don't drink today- yesterday it was the other way round. Better though. Sea like a mill pond and still patchy – haven't seen any boats since yesterday morning, perhaps its because I've looked at the wrong times.

Unusually quiet day. Mileage 321 and nothing at all exciting.

Race meeting for ORs [*Other Ranks*] and I later hung over the rail with an RAF radio operator and mechanic and had quite a chat. I am in shorts only; he couldn't place me a bit and I didn't over-enlighten him but let him do most of the talking. Interesting and good fun. Crib at night passed time satisfactorily – clocks back 30 mins – very hot below.

Sun 30th June Cooler when we awoke and didn't throw too great a sweat over breakfast. Jock and I spent a long time talking – he is interesting and has given me lots of guff about printing, his trade.

Up on deck later, we passed close to oil tanker **San Amado** Abadan–Grangemouth, going our way – we've overtaken something! At midday passed twin reefs **'The Brothers'** 80 miles South of **Gulf of Suez,** 250 miles from **Suez Bay.**

Mileage covered 318.

Should see land again this evening and be in **Suez** early tomorrow morning. Evaded church service. Immediately after lunch wrote to Connie and brought this up to date.

Land (**Egypt**) to port most of afternoon and sighted **Sinai Peninsular** in distance at 1715. Refrig Ship **Port Jackson** Fremantle–London overtook us after steadily chasing us for about 4 hours. A very smart ship and she sailed on our beam for some time holding a morse conversation with us. After dinner (1830) we were abreast of **Shetland Island** – port side- which lies in the entrance of **Suez Gulf.**

Were treated to an exquisite sunset and able to watch the sun until its 'last action had dipped below the sea horizon. At one period it made the sky into a perfect rainbow, ranging from red above the horizon where the sun had disappeared, to the blue sky above us and indigo of night behind us.

A cinema show was booked but, as we were about to sit down on our lifebelts on the deck, it was announced that the machine had broken down and they were very sorry etc – so were we! Crib again filled our time. Bed 1200. Very high wind kept us amazingly cool.

MON 1st July

A cool, almost cold night! – the best we have had on board so far: no awaking and felt properly refreshed on arising.

Just short of Suez when went on deck at 0715 and could recognise the shapes of the succeeding mountain ranges to the west as we passed them. Sea blue turned to dark green then slowly to light green, a nice restful colour. Then suddenly I was able to pick out Atarka – the vehicle assembly place, then the chimneys of Suez. The ship slowed and gradually we slipped in at breakfast time 0800.

Everything on land was quite distant and we could see the **Port Jackson** ahead of us. While eating we let go the anchor and from the saloon could see sails outside. The reason for the latter soon became apparent – we were surrounded by Gumboats! [*a small, local, propeller driven boat*].

A really hectic morning of bargaining mixed with fantastic prices being paid for leather handbags, to an assorted bunch of crooks of all nationalities, who in the most remarkable English haggled and bargained from the decks and even from the top of masts of their craft.

At 1100 we up anchored and slipped into the canal, passing the near half of a ship, a relic from the days of bombing and mining in the canal, which was floating in the inner harbour. The Port of Tawfiq and canal control offices and officers quarters looked delightful – the town of Suez itself didn't look bad but then we couldn't smell it, we were in a shady breeze and we had no flies!

The east side was nothing but rolling sand; sand to infinity; Beyond the town in the west bank area, a strip of fertility, never more than ¼ mile wide, then sand, then hills of sandstone – **Egypt!**

Our passage is limited to 10 mph through the sand and is over-marked with buoys. In places the stone walling is worn away but are constantly being repaired by ships which potter up and down on that job alone.

A huge mass of twisted, rusty steel, all that remained of yet another war victim – sunk, then dynamited, then scraped off the sand bed in small pieces smaller anyway! We went to lunch and could see sand hills and an occasional fir tree through the ports. A road runs parallel to us and it is this which is tree lined. Lunch over and was just in time to see two more piles of junk before we entered the **Bitter Lakes** [*halfway up Suez Canal*] – the vista once again delightful from a boat; my sympathy goes out to the boys who have to wave as we go by.

As we went through, I recalled many of the area's questionable pleasures and horrors. Two Italian battleships are now moored in the Great Bitter Lake and look likely to stay there.

A group of dolphins were sporting themselves in the middle, as clear as anything and looked delightfully cool. We have just sailed back into the canalled part and I'm going to look out for any parts of this diary that need updating.

Written 1830 2nd July

Lots more happened – we were passing things of interest all the time and many brought back old memories – donkeys, camels, mosques, dirty villages, clean looking towns, sand, glare, scrub, tarbouches [*a fez*] and Egyptian Army patrols on camels. We anchored for an hour at **Ismailia** to await the passing of ships travelling south. The first to arrive was the ***ORBITA***, sister ship to ours and an exact replica, even down to the search light on the bows. She was loaded with war brides bound for Australia and there was plenty of whistling and catcalling as we passed.

She was closely followed by an American tanker and the quick witted came out with a very appropriate 'Got any gum, chum'. On again, passing an Engineer School and all sorts yachting and swimming in the lakes until darkness when the searchlight came into action. Road and railway run parallel to canal and the collection of lights from headlamps, houses and buoys quite remarkable.

TUES 2nd July

We must have arrived in Port Said about midnight. When I awoke it was to the sound of the Gumboat wallahs hawking their wares. By this time, we had fuelled up and were taking on the last of the water. Whole morning was spent in watching varied antics of the super-salesmen and they must have relieved the boat of hundreds of pounds. Leather, purses, handbags, cases, wallets, dates, Turkish delight and silk like shawls of delightful patterns were hauled off in little baskets from the boats.

Dredging in progress opposite, a small aircraft carrier arrived – a Russian cargo boat left, the sun blazed, the buildings glared. We departed at 1530 and we were out in **the Mediterranean** by 1615. Made the most of the open sea and showered in clean water (can't in port).

The sand-coloured houses reflecting the sun and the heat and once again, as they dropped below the skyline, we were on our way, nothing to look at but waves and the sky. The first performance of the ships concert – later heard it was not up to much and would be better if there were no women in it! We stuck to crib!

WEDS 3rd July

Blimey its cold! I had to wake up and pull the blanket over me sometime in the night and on deck before breakfast it was definitely chilly. Heated up during day though and makes travelling much more comfortable as we can now sleep at night without soaking ourselves in perspiration.

Very quiet day – passed no ships – sunbathed, chessed, cribbed and carried on with normal chores. Boat stations filled in half an hour. 1630 crew too had an 'Emergency Stations' and fiddled around with the boats. Folks getting out service dresses and have started to polish their buttons in anticipation. Everyone more cheerful as there is a general feeling of being near home now that we are **'West of Suez'!**

THURS 4th July

Cold – on deck for the sun. **Britannic** [*four funnel transatlantic Steam Ship*] passed a couple of miles off, heading east. Cards on the deck, chess below when we decided we had had sufficient sun. A cold drink these days is really cold. The sea is so calm and the boat so steady now that there is not the slightest sensation of motion most of the time. An occasional quiver like the movement on a train is all that there is. I have to look over the side to realise that we are actually 'on our way' still. Cinema show again cancelled, much to the annoyance of all concerned.

During the afternoon, having nothing to do, I started a spit and polish session on my shoes, and it ended up with four of us doing the same thing. Crib, chess and reading are really the only things which make the time pass quickly and most of us are becoming lethargic with lack of exercise. News over radio is full of bread rationing; general chatter on board is of only one thing 'When will we arrive?'

FRI 5th July

Should pass **Malta** today but as we will be somewhat to north of the island its possible, we will see nothing. We are on the absolute shortest course from **Pt Said** in a straight line to **Cape Bon** [*Tunisia*] and then as direct as can be to **Gibraltar** – where we are told we are to call – squashing rumours of 'We are stopping', 'We are not stopping'.

More shipping about, including empty Oil tankers off to Persia. Now 1000hrs and seem to have exhausted days possibilities – fed up with reading, don't fancy chess – roll on Liverpool!! Heard that many people who bought bags etc at the Egyptian ports are now selling them owing to lack of funds.

Weather still cloudless, hazy, perfect. Mediterranean cruising in peacetime should really be good. Will try it some time when this has worn off. Fewer people sunbathing and more in the lounge (I am) playing cards etc. Spent greater part of afternoon in bunk.

Passed between **Malta and Sicily** at 1600 – both in sight, I didn't realise they were so close. Malta looks pitifully small for the bashing it took. Very pleasant up on deck after dinner, so we took up the chessmen, and played until 2130. Beautiful sunset again and a starry night to follow. Will be passing **Cape Bon** at 0600 tomorrow. Three weeks on board completed.

SAT 6th July

Gawd – it's cold! Sunbathers conspicuous by lack of numbers, I could use a pillow! Rumoured we are due to arrive 12th or 13th means today will be last Saturday, tomorrow the last Sunday and so on – a very nice feeling.

Passing thro' **Bay of Tunis** early AM and a large island jutted up on the port at breakfast time. Boat stations at 10.00 was a time filler, especially as we were then running along the North African coast – didn't look at all inviting.

Still cold and I'm keeping my jacket on today – to hell with a healthy tan. Stayed in bunk after lunch. Battle dresses for warmth appeared at night. We stuck in smokeroom until a draught (there's half a gale and a strong sea running) blew us to another spot. Several people – and Jock – seasick – at this stage! Pyjama jacket, a sheet <u>and</u> a blanket were required to bed down at night.

SUN 7th July

Woke up feeling rather warm – the wind had dropped and there was a bit of a fug in the dormitory. Nice up on deck and the sun was once again really hot.

Church service in the lounge was followed immediately at 1100 by the daily request hour of gramophone records and some of the hottest swing imaginable.

Still going along North African coast – abeam of Algiers at 1300. Made a crib board early AM which made our scoring easier and the game more comfortable. Stayed below after lunch – showers were cold and made one inclined to hurry the washing process.

A cinema show was billed for 1945 hrs, at which time it was still broad daylight. The crowd sat on their life belts on the deck for an hour before the show began and I for one was already completely cramped. Began with a short (*film*) of an ancient pseudo Spanish band – awful – and then the main film *Carolina Blues* was even worse. Stuck it out until it came to a halt to change reels then Jock and I escaped to a quieter portion of the boat and exchanged reminiscences of 'moons' over rail and orangeades. This was brought about by a perfect moonlit night sparkling over the sea, through which a merchant ship passed, busily engaged in a long morse lamp conversation with our bridge. Turned in at 2200 and again used all the bed clothes.

MON 8th July

Presenting **Spain** on our right!! Mountains right down to the sea. Another lovely day, sparkling blue sea running with us for the first time, light wind and good visibility. Sir Reg Dorman Smith [*the departing Governor of Burma*] gave a talk on Burma which failed to carry to the only place that I could find a seat, so I went out on deck again and continued to sun myself. Could see snow on Sierra Nevada at 1100. Had to queue from 1255 for a haircut at 1345! How I hate queues!

Afternoon below. Chess on deck after dinner until **Gibraltar** sighted in distance (and in the sun, so it was hard to see.) at 1930. My first glimpse made it appear like a gigantic cake with icing over the top and running down the sides – it was covered with cloud and gave the impression of being flat topped. As we approached and rounded the point of the rock so that the sun was behind us and shining on to the view, we had fine outlook – houses, guns, ships, airplane hangars and rock towering up to infinity. A good layout for our many photographers.

Anchored at about 2010 and a tender load of spit and polish soldiers boarded – cries of 'have you brought your mums with you' greeted them and they had no witticisms in return. Its suggested they are cadets returning home.

A good sunset behind the hills on the Algiers side and then Gib absolutely sparkled with lights – a wonderful sight! Really cold up on deck and we went below at 2200 as the ship got underway once again.

TUES 9th July

The Atlantic is nothing spectacular in good weather, calm sea, land – Portugal, just on the horizon all the morning. Passed two or three ships, but nothing of any great size. Boat stations and sunning ourselves on deck – we're round the bend! The last one!

Quiet afternoon, quieter evening – many more battle/ service dresses appearing. I'm keeping mine below until really necessary – I'm going to need it! Light until nearly 10 pm anyway!!

WEDS 10th July

Awoke at 0728 – the water goes off at 0730 and I missed it so had to wash and shave in a mug of water from the drinking tap. Shaved badly and raised plenty of blood in an altogether hit and miss affair.

Just in time for breakfast 0800. Still, by the time I went up on deck it was much warmer than the early birds had reported and was really pleasant.

Had to fill in a comprehensive form giving all service particulars to War Office – the beginning of the end.

Up on deck for the rest of the morning. Loudspeakers not so busy as usual and everyone ticking over at high pitch. Sunbathing PM but in evening stayed in lounge as it was too cold up on top – we all have to wear serge from tomorrow, and it should be quite comfortable. Now in **Bay of Biscay** – sea smooth but with a long swell which pushes the boat up and down a bit.

THURS 11th July

Battledress feels quite good – really cold early AM although a perfect morning. Stayed inside all the morning but went out in the sun after lunch. All final preparations now being made – due in Liverpool late Friday night and should dis-embark on Saturday. Packing will be the next problem as I've acquired several items since coming aboard and may have to dump some of the light tropical clothing to make room – we'll see about that tomorrow. If the weather at home is anything like it is here, they're having 'the best ever'.

Night cold – to us – clear and lovely – moon over the sea is something over which people are apt to break out into poetry. 23rd Day!

FRI 12th July

Sea is like a mill pond – the flattest and calmest I've ever seen. Passed through a trawler fleet, about 20 strong off **Bristol Channel** – saw **Bishop's Rock** ighthouse at 1030 – anyway it was English Territory. Rumours of times f destination are rife and throwing the pessimists into depression as the ronger story is that we don't get off till after 1800 hrs tomorrow – people are ewailing travelling, phoning etc over the weekend with holiday crowds using l the facilities – What the Hell!

And there the diary ends!

When he arrived at Liverpool he made that all important call to his 'pen-friend', Connie Pead, and they met for the first time. He had lots of leave saved up and hey made good use of it, initially meeting in the evenings after Connie finished work and later, after his discharge from the Army they had a well earned holiday n Cornwall. Things continued to progress and by the following May they were married. You'll find a picture of the happy occasion in the Appendix,

The rest as they say is history!

Bibliography

Books:

The following books were used as valuable sources of background information to the events described:

The Road Past Mandalay by John Masters, published in 1961

Battle for Burma by E.D. Smith, published in 1979

Meiktila 1945: The battle to liberate Burma by Edward M Young, published in 2004

Quotes from each of these have been highlighted within the text and are volumes which are highly recommended reading for those who want to learn more about the events described.

Various on-line sources including:

Wikipedia

The National Army Museum

The Imperial War Museum

British Military History

The BBC History, WW2, Key events.

Documents Referred to in the Text

1. December '41: Copies of Greeting cards from Egypt

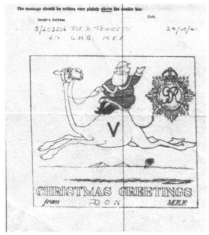

2. May '43 : Secret Orders for "The Great Trek"

```
Area Mhow.                              Genstaff.
Admin.Comdt.,Jhansi.                    Rear H.Q. Southern Army
C.C.Cawnpore.                           *Eastern Army.
Area Allahabad.                         *C.C.Dhond.
C.C.Benares.                            *Adv H.Q. Southern Army.
Lucknow District.                       101 L of C Area.
C.C.Convoy (Mhow please pass).

         * G(SD)(2) - *(G(3) - *S&T - ORD - MED.

MOVEMENT ORDER ROAD No.14.
Road Convoy (ex-Southern Army), Mhow-Benares and onward to Ranchi.
(3rd part.), 254 Bde.)

Ref: Rear H.Q. Southern Army No.4413504 of 17-5-43 (Addressees marked
* Only).

1. Germents.
   The Convoy will consist of the following personnel and vehicles:

   British:    181 Indian 218.
   Vehicles:   69 Tank Transporters 29.

   Itinerary.
2. As the tank transporters are NOT able to travel more than 80 miles
   per day the following itinerary will be follwed :-
```

Serial	Date	Stage	Mileage	Petrol	Ord/V/Shop	Hosp
1.	27 May	HALT Mhow		Yes	Yes	Yes
2.	28 May	Mhow-Shajapur.	72			
3.	29 May	Binagunj.	74			
4.	30 May	Kolaras	95			
5.	31 May	Jhansi	76	Yes	Yes	Yes
6.	1 June	HALT Jhansi.				
7.	2 June	Jhansi-ORAI ATA	88			
8.	3 June	Cawnpore	59	Yes	Yes	Yes
9.	4 June	Khaga	68			
10.	5 June	Allahabad	52	Yes	Yes	Yes
11.	6 June	HALT Allahabad				
12.	7 June	Allahabad-Benares.83		Yes	No	Yes

```
3. Staying beyond Benares will be arranged by 101 L of C Area.

   Approximate maximum distance between stages in 80 miles.  Copy of
101 L of C Area Movement Order will be sent to O.C. Convoy c/o O.C.
Benares.

4. P.O.L.
   (i) Petrol will be drawn at Mhow, Biaora, Shivpuri, Jhansi, Cawnpore
Allahabad, Benares, as necessary.
   (ii) High Speed Diesel fuel will be issued at Mhow, Jhansi,Allaha-
2500 gallons at each stage.
   (iii) Lubricants for the entire journey are being carried from L...
```

SECRET.

Ref. TT/589/SS/143
589 Tank Transporter Coy. R.A.S.(
c/o 21 Advanced Base Post Office.
Dated 22nd May 1943.

MOVEMENT ORDER. - ROAD PARTY.

INFORMATION - Company will move to new location on the 22/5/43.

INTENTION - Personnel remaining will travel by road with unit vehicles.

METHOD - Company will be divided into three sections for the move.

      H.Q. Section - Soft vehicles and spare drivers.
          (Sgt. Greenacre - C.S.M.)

      Tptrs. A-B-C Secs.- Tank Transporters and crews.   Appdi
          (Lieut. Keat.)   'A'

      W/Shops Sec.- W/Shops recovery and maintenance teams
          (Capt. George)

ORDER OF MARCH - as in Appendix 'A'.   } to follow

ROUTE - Appendix 'B'.

V.T.M.- 15   400 yards between Sub-Sections.

M.I.H.- H.Q. 15 - Transporters 12.

ADMIN - MESSING - Officer i/c Lieut. Townsend, who will make all arrangements for B.O.R's and I.O.R's, C.Q.M.S. Brown will be
responsible for daily issue.

SECURITY OF ARMS- Nominal rolls will be submitted to H.Q. by 1300hrs
22/5/43 giving numbers of arms as issued.
All ranks will be responsible for their own arms and
will sleep with them unless orders to the contrary ar
issued.
It is stressed that loss of arms is a Court Martial
offence. Officers i/c Sections will make a daily ch
of arms.

BIVOUAC - All I.O.R's will come directly under the Indian A'
immediately maintenance is finished after the day
he will be responsible for their administration
first parade next day.

DEFENCE - Lieut. Townsend will co-ordinate the defence an'
in bivouac and instruct the C.S.M. and Ind. Adj.
accordingly.

WATER - As only two Water Trucks will be available, C.S.M. wil
be responsible for strict water discipline.

3. December '44 : Copies of Greetings cards from the 14th Army

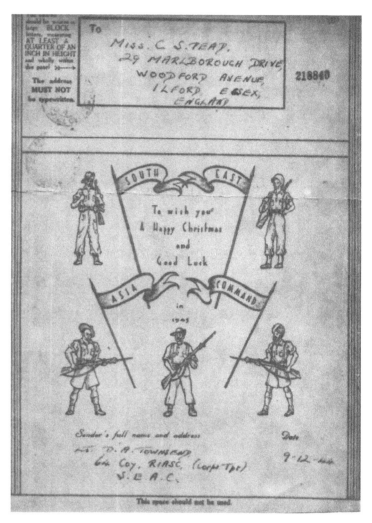

4. October '45 : Japanese Burmese currency

5. May '46 : A typical page from 'The Diary' of the trip home

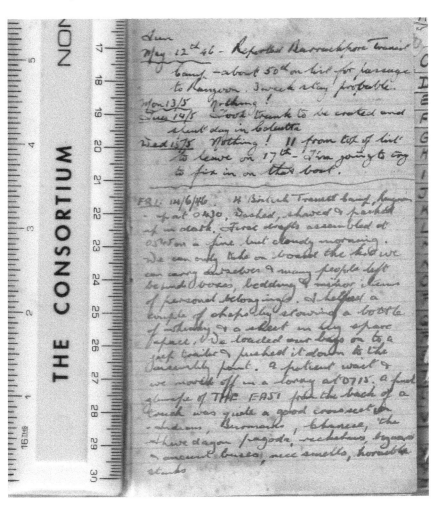

Not the easiest writing to decipher

6. May 1947: Wedding Picture – the start of another new adventure!

Lightning Source UK Ltd.
Milton Keynes UK
UKHW010624250422
402014UK00001B/80